LIFE
Your Great Adventure
A Theosophical View

**FORMERLY TITLED
THEOSOPHY: KEY TO UNDERSTANDING**

by Eunice and Felix Layton

*This publication made possible with
the assistance of the Kern Foundation*

**The Theosophical Publishing House
Wheaton, Ill. U.S.A.
Madras, India / London, England**

Originally published as *Theosophy: Key to Understanding*
©1967 The Theosophical Publishing House

©1988 The Theosophical Publishing House
Revised Edition 1988

The Theosophical Publishing House
306 West Geneva Road
Wheaton, IL 60187

A publication of the Theosophical Publishing House, a
department of the Theosophical Society in America.

Library of Congress Cataloging-in-Publication Data

Layton, Felix.
    Life, your great adventure.

    "Originally published under the title: Theosophy,
key to understanding."
    Rev. ed. of: Theosophy, key to understanding /
Eunice S. Layton. [1967]
    Bibliography: p.
    1. Theosophy. I. Layton, Eunice S. Theosophy,
key to understanding.   II. Title.
BP565.L25L54   1988   299'.934   88-40136
ISBN 0-8356-0635-X

Printed in the United States of America

LIFE
Your Great Adventure

Never forget that Life can only be nobly inspired and rightly lived if you take it bravely and gallantly, as a splendid adventure in which you are setting out into an unknown country, to face many a danger, to meet many a joy, to find many a comrade, to win and lose many a battle.

Annie Besant

Contents

Foreword

Since the teachings in this book can be of great value to those who accept them, it gives me great pleasure to introduce this publication by Eunice and Felix Layton.

As devoted Theosophists, this husband and wife team have for many years traveled throughout the world to lecture for the Theosophical Society relating ageless concepts of Theosophy to the problems of modern life. I feel sure that this book, based on some of their talks, will give to its readers the same inspiration and peace of heart and mind which so many have found in listening to them.

The basic ideas of Theosophy are written in the clear and concise manner in which the authors think and speak and write. I am grateful to these two friends for this opportunity to share in their book and to wish it Godspeed.

Geoffrey Hodson

Publisher's Preface to the Revised Edition

This revised edition of a favorite introductory book has been prepared by the publisher under the authors' supervision. The new edition has the same goal as the original—to present the essential ideas of the ancient wisdom called Theosophy in a clear, interesting, practical way. The content and language have been brought up to date where necessary. Several long chapters have been divided, their contents slightly rearranged, and the format changed in numerous other minor ways. The authors had reading lists at the end of several chapters; these have been updated and similar lists provided for all other chapters. The publisher rather than the authors, however, is responsible for the added titles in those lists.

Preface

The ideas outlined in this book are principles of the ancient wisdom taught by wise men and women of all nations and ages. These timeless laws are discussed in an attempt to show that they are deeply meaningful in relation to the events and experiences of everyday life in the twentieth century.

No claim is made that these chapters represent the basic concepts of Theosophy. We present such ideas as we have discovered in our study of the great classic Theosophical literature and in our search for the deeper meanings of life. We offer these ideas for the consideration of fellow seekers for truth in the hopes that they may be helpful, as they have been to us, in forming a more complete understanding of life.

This volume is offered in response to numerous requests from the many people we introduced to Theosophy during our years as field workers for the Theosophical Society. We hope that it may contribute something to the discovery by its readers of some of the noble and spiritual truths of that great philosophy.

1

Divine Plan in a Chaotic World

As the author Gertrude Stein lay dying, her friends gathered around her bed. Suddenly she sat bolt upright and, staring into the distance, cried out, "What is the answer?" An embarrassed silence fell like a pall upon those in the room, lasting only a few minutes, though it seemed much longer. Then Gertrude Stein sank back upon her pillow, a little smile played upon her lips, and she said, "Well, then, what is the question?"

All thoughtful people, at some period in their lives, ask themselves great sweeping questions, such as: "What is the nature of this universe?" "What is a human being?" "What essentially am I?" and "What is the purpose of life?" At all times and in all countries people have asked such searching questions, turning to the wise teachers of their nations and times for help in finding answers. They did so in ancient Greece, Egypt, Persia, India, China, and Peru. Today also, thoughtful people everywhere turn to the wise for aid in solving these great problems, and the sages give the benefit of their wisdom to the seekers.

Religion, Science, and Theosophy

The sages of today are mainly of two great classes: those of religion and those of science. Unfortunately, however, the answers of scientists often seem in conflict with the teachings of religion, and seekers are left more confused than ever. Dr. Edmund W. Sinnott, Dean Emeritus of the graduate school of Yale University, in *The Biology of the Spirit* (Viking Press), describes the dilemma in these words:

> Thoughtful people have thus been forced to lead double lives, one adapted to the practical affairs of the mechanistic world and the other to those deeper intuitive and emotional feelings which speak with such commanding inner authority.

This apparent conflict causes much distress to the earnest seeker; but it should not, for in reality there is no conflict but only two complementary viewpoints, an understanding of both of which is necessary if we are to come closer to a complete understanding of life and its mysteries. Religion and science work in different directions like the first finger and the thumb when they grasp an object, and just as the first finger or the thumb alone can only hold an object uncertainly, so an understanding of life's problems based on science or on religion alone is uncertain, whereas a problem grasped simultaneously from the two approaches of religion and science, can be firmly grasped and understood.

Such a firm grasp by the divergent movements of the finger and thumb is possible only because both are parts of a larger unit, the hand. And the firm grip on a problem which comes through using the approaches of religion and science is possible only when they are seen to be part of a greater unity which is the Ancient Wisdom. This Ancient Wisdom has been known under different names in different cultures. In India it has been and still is known as Brahma Vidya (Wisdom of Brahma); the Neo-Platonists called it Theo Sophia (God Wisdom). In modern days Theosophy presents the same great basic ideas, which unite our seeking along the lines of religion, science, art, philosophy and all other lines of humanity's search for truth. Let us try to see how the ideas and ideals of the Ancient Wisdom can bring the opposing approaches of religion and science to work in unity to answer life's greatest questions.

Science and the Three Mysteries

Let us first look at the approach of science and see how it tells the story of creation. When we consider the scientific approach, two important things stand out. The first is the method and field of investigation used by science, which limits itself to a consideration of the objective universe of matter. It starts from an examination of the world of matter, the almost endless number of different forms and combinations of properties in the world around us that we contact with our physical senses. To understand it, scientists examine this bewildering diversity of form and seek to identify the fundamental laws which unite objects and phenomena. The second important thing is the existence of three great gaps or mysteries which the scientific approach can neither bridge nor solve.

First, there is a gap between that blank or darkness, or "nothingness," before manifestation began and the time when science begins its story. The Big Bang theory is currently accepted as a partial explanation of how the universe began. Still, a mystery surrounds the question of how anything at all came from nothing.

After the inflationary period that followed the Big Bang, our sun and its planetary system began forming from a huge cloud of gas which began to collapse. The most generally accepted theory of the origin of our planets is that, after the sun was formed, the matter left over became a disk rotating around the sun, from which the planets condensed. Thus an orderly system emerged from the chaos of a gaseous cloud.

The next chapter of the scientific story of creation begins when our planet has cooled so that the dense clouds of vapor have begun to condense and form the oceans; but before this chapter can be told, a second gap or mystery in scientific knowledge has to be passed. Somewhere in those warm oceans, atoms and molecules were brought together in peculiar combinations of great complexity, and in these microscopic, yet highly complex particles, a new element appeared which we call life or consciousness.

In a sense, life and consciousness are and have always been present in every particle of matter in the universe. But it is only when organisms reach a certain degree of complexity that we recognize consciousness functioning through matter. When present, it holds the materials together and directs their activities. When it is withdrawn, at what is called death, the particles separate and disintegrate. The second great gap in science's story of creation, then, is the unanswered question of the source, the nature, and the origin of this life or consciousness that is inherent in matter. But granted that consciousness has appeared, the second chapter unfolds with fascinating

detail the story of the evolution of livir
plant and animal kingdoms.

Over millions of years, science tells us, in respo.
to the fluctuations in environment and to inner life
pressures, changes took place in the structures of
organisms. Gradually the seemingly endless variety
of living forms of the plant and animal kingdoms were
produced, each having its position either on the main
trunk or on some side branch or twig of that mighty
tree of evolution. Thus science shows, in its theory
of evolution, a vast ordered system of steady differen-
tiation from the simple to the more complex forms of
living things.

Then comes another gap or mystery, to be bridged
before the third chapter can be told. This particular
gap is so openly recognized that it is popularly though
inaccurately referred to as "the missing link," the link
between the animal and the human kingdoms.* The
origin and nature of the human element is still a
mystery, but, granted that the first human beings have
appeared on earth, then the story proceeds.

Human beings, at first, we are told, were primitive
and crude, living to satisfy their needs and urges, often
completely without regard for others. They formed
clans, tribes, and nations, and built civilizations,

---

*The term arose because some popular expressions of evolution
speak of human beings as evolving from apes and thus look for
a "missing link" between the two—evidence of a half-human,
half-ape transitional species. Evolutionists say, however, that
modern humanity and modern anthropoid apes both developed
from a common ancestor, and thus there is no "missing link."
Nevertheless, the mystery symbolized by that term remains. How
did human consciousness—so different from that of nonhuman
animals—arise?—ED

though human weakness and ignorance undermined these structures so that they crumbled or were destroyed. There was thus a rise and fall of civilizations; yet through it all there was a slow steady upward movement, a rhythmic progress, which led humanity from its primitive, cave-dwelling existence to its present state. Thus this third chapter science's story of creation shows in the human world a steady growth from primitive organization to a highly organized system.

In this story, as told by science in its efforts to answer the great fundamental questions of the universe, three things stand out. First, the story is limited to the world of matter, or to causes which produce results in the world of matter. Second, in the detailed presentation of its three chapters it shows change from simple, apparently chaotic conditions of little or no organization, to complex and highly organized systems. It shows this process repeating itself at successively higher levels like the rounds of a spiral. Third, the story has three great gaps in it, namely: the nature and origin of the subatomic particles of which the matter of the universe is built; the nature and origin of the life or consciousness that inhabits all forms; and the nature and origin of human consciousness.

Religion's Fundamental Principles

Let us now turn to the approach of religion to these fundamental questions—not the ideas of any one religion, but those ideas which are common to Buddhism, Christianity, Hinduism and the great religions of all times, the ideas which represent the essence of the religious approach. Religion sees these great basic questions from a point of view in many ways the exact opposite of that of science. Its approach is from the aspect of spirit rather than from that of matter, from an original unity rather than from an existing diversity, and from a formless world rather than from an objective world. Behind all the bewildering details of scriptural story and precept, the great religions express in diverse ways these fundamental principles:

1. There exists one supreme First Cause from which all manifestation comes forth and to which it will return. It is Eternal, Causeless, Still. It is said that "only its laws endure."

2. A fragment of the divine Self is enshrined in the heart of every living thing, seeking to unfold its divine Self through the lower nature in the world of matter. This has been called "The Inner Ruler Immortal, seated in the heart of all beings."

These concepts are examples of those "deeper intuitive and emotional feelings which speak with such commanding inner authority" of which Dean Sinnott spoke. Unfortunately, however, as time has passed, human superstitions and fears have so heavily covered these great principles with the dust and grime of human weaknesses that it is frequently difficult to perceive the realities. But they exist in all the great scriptures of the world.

Clearly there is a gap between the spiritual truths presented by religion and the objective facts described in detail by science. Leading thinkers try to bridge this gap and show these two as a part of a greater unity. For example, Albert Einstein said that science without religion is lame and religion without science is blind. He said also that he felt reverence for the illimitably superior Intelligence which reveals itself in the few details we are able to perceive.

The playwright Robert Sherwood, approaching from the opposite side of the gap, wrote:

> The most important statement in the recorded history of man is: "God created man in His own Image"... [This Divine Source] has impelled man out of the jungles and along the ascending path that leads to the stars...his perhaps blind, but persistent faith in his God-like qualities has enabled man to defy all scientific proof that he is frail, physicallly and morally— that he is in a word, mortal. He has gone out on his own and found ways to make himself immortal.

Theosophy's Key to the Three Mysteries

At the end of the last century H. P. Blavatsky, who introduced Theosophy to the modern world, made a statement which bridged science and religion when she said: "Wherever there is an atom or a particle of matter there is life in it." This idea, that there is both a life and a form aspect in all creation, is a concept that can link science and religion.

Suggested in this thought is one of the great basic ideas of Theosophy. It gives a key to a deeper understanding of life's great questions. It is the concept that all manifestation is dual, that it has two aspects, spirit and matter, or life and form, and that in order to understand nature we must appreciate both. We must see both the life and the form in all things. From this point of view the facts of science are seen to be only one side of the picture, the form side. We must look at the life side as well.

In the first chapter of science's story of creation, we saw in the world of form the emergence of a solar system from a chaotic, gaseous nebula. This is a wonderful description of the form side of the picture, with vast changes in the world of matter. Walt Whitman, in his poem "When I Heard the Learn'd Astronomer," describes the far deeper understanding which comes by appreciating, not only the development and changes of form described by astronomy, but the life side as well:

> When I heard the learn'd astronomer,
> When the proofs, the figures, were ranged in columns
> before me,
> When I was shown the charts and diagrams, to add,
> divide, and measure them,
> When I sitting heard the astronomer where he lectured
> with much applause in the lecture-room,
> How soon unaccountable I became tired and sick,
> Till rising and gliding out I wandered off by myself,
> In the mystical moist night-air, and from time to time,
> Look'd up in perfect silence at the stars.

One who has thus stood alone, looking at the stars in perfect silence, knows that in the cosmos, in addition to the material universe, a life-force throbs through space seeking to express itself ever more fully as matter becomes more and more responsive to the great life-forces of the universe.

In the second chapter of creation, the lowly forms of the plant kingdom, such as the algae, lichen and mosses, are limited channels for the expression of the life within; but as each higher stage is reached, life expresses itself more completely until it is most fully seen in the grandeur and majesty of a great tree or the beauty of a flower. Similarly, in the animal kingdom, life can express itself only feebly in the simpler forms of the mollusk and jellyfish. The forms of fishes, amphibians, reptiles and mammals become more responsive to the divine life until it reaches yet higher expression in the grace and beauty of a deer and the loyalty, devotion, and intelligence of some of our domestic animals and pets, such as the horse, the dog, and the cat.

In our species also, at first the life and form were very incompletely drawn together in the primitive human. As time passed a stage of advancement was reached in which the divine life expressed itself somewhat more fully in so-called civilized people, who are still far from perfect. Here and there, however, as we read the history of the world, we find instances in which human beings have so molded the matter of their personality that it has become an almost perfect expression of the life within. They are the great leaders of humanity, our sages and our saints.

Thus, each chapter of science's story repeats the same theme: life descending to express itself more fully through the form, and the form becoming ever more complex and better adapted to express the life within. It is as though the world of form sought slowly to mold itself into a chalice to receive the outpouring of the divine life. This process repeats itself at successively higher levels in the spiral of evolution.

For Further Reading:

Atoms, Snowflakes and God, by John Hitchcock
Dialogues with Scientists and Sages, by Renée Weber
Science, Yoga and Theosophy (a collection of papers)
Understanding through the Ancient Wisdom and Modern Science, by Alfred Taylor
Visual Meditations on the Universe, by James S. Perkins

2

Evolution on the Three Paths

The key idea of the dual unfoldment of matter and consciousness in the manifest cosmos gives added meaning and significance to our study of the great processes of the macrocosm, but what about individuals like you and me? How does this knowledge affect us?

The connection between the universe and the individual becomes apparent when we think of the great "Principle of Correspondences," which states that the great cosmic processes reflect themselves, in miniature, in the processes of individuals. The principle, as it relates to humanity was stated by Swedenborg when he said that the entire creation is a titanic being, and we are made in the image and likeness of the universe. The Chinese philosopher Lao-tze said the universe is a human being on a large scale. The converse of this is: A human is the universe on a small scale. Tennyson stated this idea in poetic form when he said of the flower:

. . .but *if* I could understand

What you are, root and all, and all in all,
I should know what God and man is.

The same principle was expressed by Dr. Alfred
Taylor of the University of Texas, in a lecture on cell
life in which he repeated over and over again, "The
whole is in the part," meaning that in the structure
and action of each cell the history and principles of
all cell life can be found.* Human beings, then, reflect
in their microcosmic world the macrocosmic principles.

Spirit and Matter Joined

A fine definition of humanity calls us that being in
the universe in whom highest spirit and lowest matter are joined together by intelligence. Slowly the life
and form in each of us draw together, the matter of
the personality becoming more responsive to the
divine life within, and the divine Self learning to express itself more and more fully through the limitations of the personality.

As we consider this concept of ourselves, however,
and then look at our daily lives, most of us will recognize that a large share of our activities are semi-
automatic responses of the lower nature to stimuli
from without, to the necessity of providing food, clothing, and shelter for the physical body, and for getting
along with our neighbors. Apparently in the physical
world we are largely unconscious of the divine Self.

Yet each of us has had moments of inspiration when
we have transcended the personality and have become

---

*Similarly, the physicist David Bohm maintains that the pattern
of the whole world is contained in each of its parts, that we live
in a holographic universe.—ED

aware of our divine nature. Such moments may have come from a deep appreciation of the beauties of nature. Perhaps as we have watched a sunset, we have known in our inmost hearts the reality of the life that pulses through this beauty and have felt a yearning to be one with it. At such a moment we have felt our inmost nature. These moments of inspiration and true Self-knowledge may have come in various ways. Perhaps they came in some great religious experience or in appreciating or creating a work of art or music. Perhaps they came in a feeling of deep, pure love, either for all humanity or for one individual. Perhaps they came in the pure joy which follows after having performed an act of service for another, without any selfish motive and at cost of real sacrifice on our part. However they may have arisen, each of us has such recollections in our own experience, and these are the moments when we have known the divine Self, the "Inner Ruler Immortal, seated in the heart of all beings."

When we think of our true spiritual nature, and of the joy which comes when we are aware of it, and compare that awareness with the life of daily routine, in which this spiritual consciousness is largely covered over by the automatic responses of the lower personality, we may well compare human nature with the symbol of the crucifix and the story of the crucifixion. In that symbol, the cross, with its four arms, represents matter—resistant, unyielding matter. Nailed to it is the most spiritual being of whom his followers can conceive, the Christ. In that symbol, matter seems to be completely triumphant, to have completely destroyed the spiritual Self which is "crucified, dead and buried." But the story goes on to tell that, though at that stage the Life seems to be overcome by matter, this is only apparent; for after he had thus descended, he "rose from the dead" and through his descent into matter, gained the capacity to serve humanity, to teach, to heal, and to bless as never before.

The gospel account is a story of the descent of the divine into every human life, its apparent death and burial in the material world and its inevitable final triumphant resurrection. In all the great religions of the world the same story is repeated in different forms. It was told in ancient Egypt as the death of the great god Osiris and his final resurrection. It is depicted symbolically in the ceremonies of Masonic orders, and it was told in Greece as the descent of Orpheus into the underworld.

A beautiful symbolic representation of the same idea is found in the meditation room in the United Nations Building in New York City. Here, where some have wisely thought it good to provide a special room where delegates may escape from the war of tongues and have "a center of stillness surrounded by silence," a problem arose as to what to put in the room, since the symbol of any religion might be inspiring to one and objectionable to another. This problem was solved by placing in the center a solid block of iron ore, symbol of matter, with a single bright light, symbol of Spirit, shining on it from above. The meaning of this is explained as the light of Spirit shining on matter and drawing forth the life within. An interesting summary of the whole idea is the statement of the philosopher Henri Bergson that "the Universe is a machine for making Gods."

The ancient teaching to be found, however much disguised, in all religions is that each human life is divine in its essential nature. That divine Self, the true inner reality, is veiled in successively denser layers of matter, each with its separate characteristics and consciousness. The ultimate purpose of life is to let this divine Self unfold and express its powers through these veils of matter—to let the beauty of the spiritual Self open, like the bud of a flower, and expose its beauty and shed its fragrance on all around.

Three Concepts from Science

The expression of the divine Self in matter, many believe, is the real purpose and ultimate goal of our life. Yet as we look at the world we see millions of people growing up, passing through youth and maturity to old age and death, without achieving this goal. Their efforts appear largely to be lost. Many feel that the teachings of religion alone are inadequate to explain this apparent failure. However, when we add the teachings of science to those of religion, we find great concepts which remove the difficulties.

First, science teaches that the process of the growth and unfoldment of the potentialities of life and form is vast and magnificently slow. Evolutionary development stretches over millions of years, sometimes seeming inactive for long periods, then suddenly surging ahead. So the individual who expects the goal of the unfoldment of spiritual powers in the world of form to be achieved in a lifetime is, to quote a Chinese saying, like one who "looks at an egg and expects to hear it crow!" Vast periods of time are required for the attainment of great goals.

The thoughtful person will then ask how such vast periods of time are to be made available if we have only one lifetime in which to achieve, and only in very rare cases does this lifetime extend to a hundred years. The answer is found in science's second great concept, that wherever life and form are united, that is, wherever there is a living thing, rhythms of various frequencies are necessary to link life and form, to maintain life. There are the extremely rapid vibrations such as electrical impulses in the brain waves investigated in encephalography and similar studies; the slower vibrations of the beating of the heart and breathing; far slower still, the endless rhythm of eating, digesting, and feeling hunger; and the rhythm of fully conscious activity during the day followed by a period of withdrawal of consciousness in sleep at night. The stopping of any of these rhythmic processes may cause death. These are only some of the more rapid vibrations. There are far longer and deeper vibrations which we lose sight of because of our preoccupation with this brief but, to us, all-important, period of time between birth and death, which we call life.

Many people feel that the growth of the immortal Self toward its goal of expression in form is by vast rhythmic processes. Just as the personality moves toward its major goals in life through many days of working and experiencing, followed by nights of rest, so on a vaster scale the immortal Self within us moves toward its great goal by its "days" of activity, which we call lives, followed by "nights" of rest, which are the periods between lives.

Thus, over vast reaches of time, commensurate with those postulated by science for the attainment of the goals of evolution, the immortal Self unfolds its spiritual powers in the world of form. This rhythmic process of the unfoldment of our divine powers has been openly avowed by great thinkers of the world when the intellectual climate has permitted. It has been hinted at, or spoken of in veiled terms, when religious orthodoxy has denied it.

Yet a third concept from the world of science must be applied to the teachings of religion to make them more deeply significant: we live in a world of law, and nature is conquered by obedience to nature's laws. Thus the unfoldment of our divine powers in these lower worlds of form takes place by a process of learning nature's laws of the physical, emotional, and mental worlds and living in accordance with them. When we have found these laws and built our lives in accordance with them, the whole of life becomes a song of happiness for ourselves and for all around us, and life expresses itself freely, beautifully, and joyously in all our actions. Thus the existence of completely inviolable natural law provides the means whereby, through vast rhythmic processes over great periods of time, the spiritual Self within us expresses itself ever more fully.

This stupendous concept—the steady growth into unity and harmonious expression of life and form until, so far as human evolution is concerned, perfection is reached—gives meaning to the words of the Christ: "Be ye therefore perfect, even as your Father in Heaven is perfect" (Matt. 5:48), and to those of Saint Paul: "Till we all come, in the unity of the faith, and of the knowledge of the Son of God, unto a perfect man, unto the measure of the stature of the fullness of Christ" (Eph. 4:13). Here are definite statements of the goal toward which all humanity is moving. It is the same goal which is described in all the religions of the world. The steps and the obstacles on the path have been pictured over and over again in allegory, in the great myths and legends of the world. In these we often find humanity symbolized by a hero or heroine with a god for father and a mortal for mother, so that they are half-mortal and half-divine—an apt picture of human nature. The stories tell how this hero or heroine sets out on a great quest and meets obstacles and overcomes them. These are symbolic of the obstacles we meet on the path, the sources of difficulty, and the help that comes from within us and around us.

In reality the path is threefold, as our true nature, being made in the divine image, is threefold. There are three major branches along which we may move toward the great goal of human perfection. These correspond to the development of the three divine attributes of will, intelligence, and love.

The Path of Will

They tread the path of will "who mould their image in the likeness of the will of God." On this path the power aspect of the threefold divine nature is dominant.

In the early stages of rhythmic growth toward perfection, the power aspect will reflect itself strongly in the personality of the seeker. Because the personality is ignorant of the laws of the worlds of form, this will and strength are directed largely to the gaining of selfish ends. Individuals in the early stages of their pilgrimage through the world of matter, use their strength to gain by force what they want, and will often satisfy their desires with great ruthlessness. This frequently makes them the center of quarrels and fights as their growing strength brings them into repeated conflict. They become petty leaders, gathering about them followers who, while respecting power, nevertheless follow primarily for what they themselves can gain by working with the powerful.

Eventually, after long periods of struggle to control their surroundings and bring to the little personality what it wants, a growing dissatisfaction dawns. Those on the path of power begin to realize that the ceaseless search for happiness and security, taking what they want by force, does not give lasting happiness but only leads to further struggle and conflict. Then, inwardly they begin the search for a deeper meaning, for that which will give lasting peace and bliss. This inner discontent slowly grows while the seeker looks deeper and deeper for the answers to life's fundamental problems.

Eventually the light begins to dawn for such persons of will. They begin to recognize that behind the chaotic turmoil there exists One Will, which is the supreme Will, and they realize slowly that the only way they can find true happiness is by putting their little wills into complete harmony with the One Will and saying: "Not my will, but thine be done."

This becomes now their goal in life, involving a complete change of motive for every feeling, thought, and action, therefore bringing about deep inner struggle. They face this task in the manner typical of the person of will. They pass the whole of their lower nature before them in review, much as a general preparing for battle might review the army. They look at their own personalities directly and fearlessly, seeing what is good that must be used and strengthened and what is wrong that must be altered or discarded. Then begins the internal conflict as they effect these changes. Violent and intense is the inner struggle, for these are persons in whom the conscious patterns of reaction have been strengthened by long effort far beyond similar efforts of others. However, they will find that, although the resistance to be overcome is greater, so also is the power within them, and, as they say: "Not my will, but thine be done," they invoke an irresistible force.

Slowly the personality is molded to become a vehicle for the expression of the One Will. Those whose will has been so transformed again emerge as leaders in the world of form, but now they are leaders in great movements for the progress of the race and for the uplifting of humanity. They are reformers—the champions of the downtrodden, the mistreated, and the victims of social injustice. They are leaders who inspire others to follow them, not by rousing the hope of selfish gain but by helping others to know and to feel the one life in all and to work in harmony with that and for its service.

For each path there is an invocation which seems particularly to call on the aspect that is its keynote. The following invocation may be helpful to followers of this path:

> More radiant than the sun,
> Purer than the snow,
> Subtler than the ether,
> Is the Self, the Spirit within my heart.
> I am that Self. That Self am I.

The Path of Wisdom

They tread the path of Wisdom "who mould their image in the likeness of the wisdom of God." Before they realize that their purpose in life is to shed around themselves the light of the wisdom of God, those who follow this path are at work in the realms of knowledge for their own ends. Cleverness and even cunning are prominent characteristics, and those who have them will take great pains to examine, analyze, and dissect, and thus will develop highly the powers of mind. The cunning lawyer and the crooked salesperson are early types of those who will progress along this line. The time will come when such people will realize that all this search for knowledge, with themselves as the center, with analysis as the method, and personal gain as the object, does not bring happiness.

Darkness and light have always been the symbols of ignorance and wisdom, and seekers for Wisdom now take light as the object of their search. The finding and spreading of the light becomes the central purpose of their lives. They now examine themselves to see where the veils of superstition and prejudice have wound about their minds and hearts blocking the light. They seek to tear down these veils and to find the light of the temple of wisdom within themselves.

Their first step is to raise their objectives from the seeking of mere knowledge to the seeking of wisdom. To do this they must leave the restless prodding and searching for details and learn to hear the unity of nature's song. They hear this ever more fully as they learn to sense the beauty and the unity of God's plan in the world and find themselves not only a part of that unity but one with it. They find deep within themselves the same light of God's wisdom which shines through all. Henceforth all their seeking and painstaking thought will be directed to finding the one light, the divine light, within themselves and in all nature. No longer will they be destructive in their search for knowledge, for now they will see directly and will invoke the light of divine wisdom within themselves to shine through the darkness of the outer forms and show them the divine light in all that they seek to understand.

As the search for the light begins to achieve success they can return to their books and the details of their worldly work and shed a wonderful new light on every problem. But they must dedicate their work utterly to the service of humanity and of the light; otherwise, the pride of the lower self, the great danger to those of this temperament, will block the shining of the light and turn them from the path they have chosen, changing light to darkness. If they hold fast to their ideals, attacks will only intensify their search until they become as a light shining in the darkness, shedding the light of God's wisdom on the world and calling to all others to rend the veils of prejudice and superstition which shroud the light within.

This invocation might be suitable for those who seek to tread the path of wisdom:

> From the unreal, lead me to the Real,
> From darkness, lead me to Light,
> From death, lead me to Immortality.

The Path of Love

They tread the path of Love "who mould their image in the likeness of the love of God." In the early stages their activities are largely dominated by the emotional nature, by its ever-changing likes and dislikes in the worlds of form. As time passes, through the experience of many lives, the emotional power becomes strong and dominates the mind and the physical body. Its desires are basically selfish and degrade both the lover and the object of affection. Finally they realize that lasting happiness will never come by gratifying the desires of the personality. Like those on the other paths, those following the way of Love enter the period of inner search, seeking a deeper goal and a deeper meaning of life. Their answer comes as they learn the universality of the life behind and within all forms, and determine to see it and serve it within their own hearts and in all forms around them, no matter how imperfect those forms may appear on the surface.

Like the others, these seekers then examine their personalities, recognizing their strong points and their weaknesses and seeking to make their personalities instruments for serving the one life within and without. The method by which they proceed is that of recognizing, even in faults, the seeds of virtues, and then giving all their attention and energy to strengthening these seeds, which will grow and blossom while, from lack of attention, the outer husk of the vice falls lifeless and in its place stands the beauty of the noble virtue.

As aspirants learn to see behind the forms to the one life, a change takes place within their own nature and they learn to live in constant inner communion with the one life within their own hearts, which steadily radiate an impersonal love on all, untroubled by the passing waves of personal feeling which no longer disturb that eternal peace. Thus they pass to their goal.

This invocation might be of particular help to those who seek to move along the path of Love:

> O Hidden Life! vibrant in every atom,
> O Hidden Light! shining in every creature,
> O Hidden Love! embracing all in oneness,

May all who feel themselves as one with thee
Know they are therefore one with every other.

It is well for each of us to decide for ourselves which
of these three paths is the path we will tread and to
begin consciously to develop the qualities of that path
now. But each should also realize that the strong development of any one of these aspects of our nature
will necessitate a development of the other two, and
the final goal of perfected humanity will be reached
only when each of us has developed all three aspects
to perfection.

For Further Reading:

The Future Evolution of Man, by Sri Aurobindo
Seven Schools of Yoga: An Introduction, by Ernest
  Wood
The Three Paths, by Annie Besant
The Transforming Mind, by Laurence Bendit and
  Phoebe Bendit

3

Your Dynamic Powers

If we need to know one thing more than anything else today, it is something about our own nature. Isn't it amazing that the last thing we discover is ourselves? As one of our military leaders has said, "We know so much about killing and so little about living. . . . We know so much about things and so little about ourselves. . . . We are a nation of nuclear giants and ethical infants."

The Search for the Self

If we look at modern knowledge and see some of the vast strides that have been taken in various fields, we will see how relatively little we know about ourselves. In the fields of astronomy and physics, scientists are continually making new discoveries. Our concepts of the universe and space and time have changed tremendously in the last hundred years. At the opposite end of the scale—look at the world of matter, the atom, the microcosm. Our ideas about matter have been revolutionized in the last century. We are getting much closer to the truth of what matter and the atom really are. How our material lives are being changed in this nuclear era! Even as far as living things are concerned, we have made progress. Through our studies of the plant and animal kingdoms, we are now able to raise a better ear of corn, a more beautiful flower, a more productive fruit tree, and more highly bred animals. We are even experimenting with genetic engineering.

But what about human nature? Most people are not only a mystery to themselves but they are even unaware that there is a mystery. Of course we cannot do much about solving a problem until we at least realize there is a problem to be solved. If we were to ask people we met on the street what they really are—what happens when they act and feel and think, what is the constant urge or driving force that makes them continue through life—not only would they be unable to answer, but the very question would seem strange to them.

Yet what can be more strange than that we travel the weary road from birth to death with all of its problems and difficulties and never stop to question why. Suppose we saw several individuals struggling up a mountain-side carrying heavy burdens, and when we stopped them to ask where they were going with such heavy loads, they were to answer that the question had never occurred to them. We would certainly think there was something wrong with those individuals. Isn't that what we are doing when we go through this life, with all of its ups and downs, and never ask why?

However, the time does come for all of us, in this long pilgrimage from birth to perfection, when we do begin to question. Such times usually come when we have experienced some great suffering or difficulty or problem—some experience that strips some of the superficiality from us and brings us face to face with ourselves—circumstances that break through these outer shells we all build around our real selves. We never question the good fortune that comes to us. We are sure we deserve anything good that comes our way—we take it all for granted; but when trouble comes, that is a different story. Clergymen, doctors, psychiatrists, and others consulted by people in trouble, will tell you that the commonest question asked by those who come for help is "Why should this happen to me?" Sometimes these great difficulties, these so-called evils, are in reality great blessings because they force us deeper within ourselves for the answers to life. One philosopher has put it this way: "Pain makes us think; thinking makes us wise; wisdom makes life endurable." However, we might change that last phrase to read: "Real wisdom makes life a great joy."

Our Three Bodies

Now let us think through this question and see if we cannot come to a little deeper understanding of what we really are. When we look at an individual, the first thing we are usually conscious of is the *physical body*—this thing we see in the mirror. Many people think they are just a physical body and that physical existence is the only existence; so they spend their entire lifetime feeding and indulging the physical body—providing it with every comfort, adorning it with costly jewels and expensive clothing, catering to its every whim. These are the persons who "live to eat," instead of "eating to live." Their philosophy is "Eat, drink, and be merry, for tomorrow we die." Such individuals are apt to have as their greatest goal in life the gaining of enough wealth to provide them with every possible luxury. But surely a little thought on the subject will convince us that we are more than merely a physical body.

In the first place, physiologists tell us that the materials of which our physical bodies are composed are constantly changing and that within a very short time we have a practically new physical body—hardly a single cell of the old one is left. Yet, we feel we are the same individuals with the same likes and dislikes, the same capacities and characteristics. Also, we can control our physical bodies—we can make them move when we want them to move, we can train them in skills, such as playing the piano or typing or swimming. Well, if I can control this physical body then I must be something more than just the physical body. Who, then, is this "I" that controls it?

Just as we have different gradations of physical matter—the solids and liquids that are visible, and air, and further gradations called "etheric," which are invisible—so there are even finer grades of matter. Thus we have what we might call emotional matter because it is subtle enough to respond to those more rapid rates of vibration we call emotion. This matter makes up our *emotional body,* sometimes called the desire body, because it is the driving force of our nature that impels us to go after the things we desire.

It is fairly easy to prove to ourselves the existence of our emotional body if we can be objective about it. The next time you have occasion to visit a funeral parlor, a hospital, a great cathedral, a football game, or an exciting movie, observe yourself and see how difficult it is, when you are in such an intense emotional atmosphere, not to let your own emotional body respond to it. It is very difficult to stay in such highly charged surroundings without beginning to feel that same type of emotion. Also, probably you have had the experience at some time in your life of being carried away by your emotions—perhaps in a fit of anger or fear or excitement—until you lost control of yourself entirely and didn't know what you were doing. However, we *can* control our emotions. So, who is the "I" who controls them?

The gradations of matter go on to finer, subtler and rarer matter capable of responding to the even more rapid vibration we call thought, and we have what we might call a *mental body* made up of this mental matter—mind stuff—so subtle and so rarefied that it is able to respond to thought waves. The concept of this "mind stuff" or mental matter offers a reasonable explanation for telepathy and other latent human powers for which J. B. Rhine, of Duke University, and many others have provided ample evidence.

Here again, we can prove to some extent for ourselves the existence of the mental body. How often, for example, do two people think of the same thing at the same time—especially if those two individuals are very close to each other. Husband and wife or two close friends who have built up a strong rapport with each other often demonstrate this coincidence of thought. One may have been thinking of something else entirely, and all of a sudden both say the same thing at the same time. Or you may have had the experience that many of us have had, of attending a lecture or class in which a professor was expounding some very profound and difficult subject. While you were listening, you seemed to comprehend the whole subject. Later, however, when you tried to explain it

to someone else, you found that you could not. When
you had only your own mental body and thought
power to apply to the subject, you were not capable
of reproducing that kind of thinking. You were able
to understand originally only because of the intense
mental atmosphere created by that professor and the
other students in the group who were following the
discussion.

Also, we can control our minds. We can concentrate on one particular problem, or turn the mind to
another subject, or hold it so still that the brain brings
through no thought images. If we can control our
mind, then we must be something more than mind.
Who, then, is this "I" that controls?

Bodies and Personality

These three bodies make up our personality: the
physical, composed of physical matter capable of responding to physical stimuli; the emotional, formed
of finer matter capable of responding to the more rapid
vibrations of emotion; and the mental, made of still
subtler and more rarefied matter capable of responding to the much more rapid vibrations of thought. The
word "personality" comes from the Latin word *per-
sona*, meaning a mask. That is exactly what the personality is, a mask of the real self—simply three cloaks
or vehicles we wear in order to experience or respond
to stimuli in three worlds of matter—physical, emotional, and mental. If we did not have these cloaks
or vehicles we could not respond to these worlds. It
is very much as if you put on a fine silk coat (the mental body), and on top of that a heavier topcoat (the
emotional body), and on top of that a huge bulky cloak
(the physical body). Each one of these limits you. Each
one of them hides the real you. Each one of them
makes it more difficult for you to express yourself as

you really are. It also makes it more difficult for others to know the real you.

Now the really great tragedy occurs when we become so limited, so encased within these cloaks or vehicles or masks, that we begin identifying ourselves with them: when we say "I am hungry" or "I am tired," we think we are really hungry and tired instead of realizing it is only the physical body that is hungry and tired; certainly we must see that it gets proper care, but is not indulged. We are even getting to the point these days of identifying ourselves with our automobiles. We hear people say "I need gas" or "I have a flat tire" or "My brakes need relining." Well, of course, we don't need gas or have flat tires; our cars do, and certainly we need to take proper care of them. The same thing is true of the body. We are no more our bodies than we are our cars. Both are vehicles we use. We make the same mistake of identifying ourselves with our emotions or thoughts. We say "I am angry" or "I am sad." You never get angry or sad—your emotional body may, but not you. You may use a car if you are going to travel on land and may change to a ship to travel the seas and a plane to travel by air. You are the same person traveling; you simply use a different vehicle depending on how you wish to travel. You are not the car or the ship or the plane; they are simply the vehicles without which you could not travel in the various elements. In just the same way, we require vehicles or bodies in order to act in the three worlds of matter. All are transient— our instruments, wearing out and being renewed according to our needs. Well then, who am I?

Evolution of Body and Spirit

To approach this question, let us consider human evolution. In your imagination picture standing beside

you the most primitive human-like being you can conceive, one of the first humanoids whose remains an-
thropologists have discovered in east Africa. Then
picture, on the other side of you, the most perfect
human being you can conceive, some great sage or
saint or spiritual king. Now compare the two. Compare them physically—this crude, stooping, unrespon-
sive physical body contrasted with this delicately
formed, beautiful, sensitive physical body. Compare
them emotionally. Compare them mentally. Compare
them morally. Compare them spiritually and in every
other way. How can you say to these two individuals,
"Be ye therefore perfect, even as your Father in
Heaven is perfect," and expect that to occur in one
lifetime? It may happen to the great being you have
pictured, but surely it is impossible for the primitive
one. How are you going to change the primitive being into the great being?

That process of change is accomplished in very
much the same way that you change an infant into
a mature adult. The infant contains within itself the
full potential of the adult, but that potential is latent—
it is germinal. It needs time and experience and proper environment in which to unfold the adult capacity. In just the same way the primitive contains the full
potential of the saint, only undeveloped, with the capacity latent instead of in full flower. How, then, does
the infant progress to adulthood? Children spend approximately (and these figures are approximate and
flexible) the first seven years of life developing and
learning to control and use the physical body—to
walk, to talk, to move their arms and keep their
balance, learning to hold or grasp things, and many
other physical skills. They eat, sleep, and play, and
such actions constitute life at this age. They spend

approximately the next seven years having a wonderful time in activity with these newly acquired skills of the physical body; all who have had contact with children know the tremendous physical activity of these years.

It is at this time that the child begins the struggle of developing the emotions. This is the adolescent age, which many find so difficult. For approximately the next seven years the adolescent experiences great emotional expansions—falling in love, "getting religion," discovering the beauties of nature or art or music. It is during this time that unfoldment of the mind begins. Adolescents now reach the age when they know so much that fathers and mothers can tell them nothing, teachers can tell them nothing—they just know it all and there is nothing anyone can tell them. Finally, they develop the mind and become mature adults who will eventually attain wisdom.

Now look at the great family of humanity and see if there are not individuals at each of these stages. There are still some infants—young souls—who are fully occupied with developing at the physical level. They are interested simply in eating and sleeping, engaging in a little physical work or activity, responding to physical stimuli, and this is the extent of life for them. Perhaps most of humanity is at the adolescent level. Look at humanity and see if the main interests of the mass of people do not lie at this emotional level. What do people turn to as soon as the pressure of earning a living lets up? What do people do when they have leisure? What is the first thing they think of? Is it not having fun, experiencing a new thrill or emotional excitement of some kind? We find a few individuals, in comparison with the whole, at the next level—the level of developing the mind. They know so much and are so proud and confident of what they know that no one can tell them anything—a characteristic of this lower mind level of development. Here and there we come across rare individuals who are the mature adults of humanity, who have developed a little real wisdom.

The child must go through the elementary grades and then to high school and on to college. At various levels of education, the student masters a number of subjects, for example, by working in a chemistry laboratory to learn chemistry, in an art studio to learn art, and on an athletic field to learn sports. So on a far larger scale the reincarnating human soul has many lifetimes, each of which is just one day in the world school, to master the lessons of life—first in one culture and then another, in one nation and then another, in this religion and that, in different races, different sexes, at different social levels. Thereby we develop all capacities and learn all the lessons in this world school.

As you think of perfected human beings you will realize that they have, balanced within themselves, all capacities. They have those qualities we think of as masculine and those we think of as feminine, those we think of as Eastern and those we think of as Western. They can respond to all peoples, be at home in all circumstances, in any environment, because they have completed life's school, learned all its lessons, and unfolded all their capacities.

Just as we begin tomorrow where we leave off tonight, so in this world school whatever capacity we unfold in one life is ours for all time. As we live this life today, so we face its consequences tomorrow or on some other tomorrow. We progress in a world of absolute law, absolute order, and absolute justice according to good common sense and reason until we have completed life's school.

We find, if we look around, that we ourselves, and everyone else, stand somewhere between the primitive and the perfected being. Primitives have within themselves all that the saint has. They are simply younger. It is no discredit to be primitive any more than it is for one child to be in the first grade while another is graduating from the university. The first-grader simply started later, that is all, but will one day reach university status too, after having had the time to unfold, and the same is true of the primitive also.

For Further Reading:

The Etheric Body of Man, by Laurence Bendit and Phoebe Bendit
Man and His Bodies, by Annie Besant
Man Visible and Invisible, by C. W. Leadbeater
Spirals of Growth, by Dwight Johnson

4

Life Unfolding in Matter

To understand what we really are and what our true destiny is, we need to gain a greater perspective—we need to build a larger framework into which we can fit all of life and through which we can see our relationship to the rest of life. Science gives us some partial answers, philosophy gives us some partial answers; religion and psychology give us partial answers, but very often the answer of the scientist seems to be in conflict with that of the philosopher; and that of the religionist doesn't agree with that of the psychologist.

Trying to fit all of these fragments of truth together is like trying to add one-third, one-fourth, and one-fifth. How are you going to add one-third, one-fourth, and one-fifth? It can never be done as long as they remain in this form—fractions with differing denominators. They can be added only when you supply a common denominator, which will be larger than any single denominator, but which will contain them all—in this case sixty. For the questions of life, a larger denominator into which we can fit all of the fragments of truth is Theosophy—the Ancient Wisdom.

In the next few pages we will, very briefly and sketchily, build a framework of Theosophy large enough to contain all of life so that we may see our relationship to it. Now, when we say "briefly and sketchily" you will understand something of what we mean when you realize that the word "Theosophy" means "divine wisdom," which none of us has in anything even approximating completeness. All the Theosophy written so far is only a fragment of a fragment of the full divine wisdom. Even to try to comprehend that which has been expressed in books, however, takes a lifetime of study, yet we are going to try to build this framework in a few pages. Obviously it will be sketchy with many gaps—just the framework or scaffolding from which you will have to erect your own edifice. Also, keep in mind that these are simply ideas and concepts for your consideration and never dogmas for your belief; they are possible hypotheses that you may want to think about and try out for yourselves.

The Evolution of Matter

Let us try to push back in imagination to a time when there was no life on this planet—no planet, no universe—just an absolute, perfect, unmanifest Deity, Causeless Cause, Logos, God, or simply *THAT*, to use the Hindu term. Of this state H. P. Blavatsky's *Secret Doctrine* says: "Time was not for it lay asleep in the infinite bosom of Duration. . . . Alone the one form of existence stretched, boundless, infinite, causeless in dreamless sleep. . . . The visible that was, and the invisible that is, rested in Eternal Non-Being the One

Being.'' It is impossible for us with finite minds to imagine the infinite, so let us begin with the process of manifestation, which is finite. Even this will seem beyond the furthest stretch of our imagination, but as we must begin somewhere, let us try this.

Some people find it easier to understand these tremendous abstract concepts with the help of diagrams and charts. The accompanying diagram is often used by Theosophists to represent the manifestation of the universe. Keep in mind, however, that it is a diagrammatic representation. Although it depicts layers of matter, one on top of another, all these are in reality right here, interpenetrating—not in layers at all. This gradation of matter could be just as truly represented by a point in the center of concentric circles such as might form if we were to drop a stone in a quiet pool—circles radiating from the point where the stone hit the water. All types of matter interpenetrate at any point, but they have been separated in layers in this diagram in order to help us understand more easily.

At the top of the diagram three circles represent the three aspects of the Divine. In Christian terminology they are referred to as God the Father, God the Son, and God the Holy Spirit. In ancient Egypt they were referred to as Osiris, Horus, and Isis. In Hinduism they are called Brahma, Vishnu, and Shiva. Because we are probably more familiar with the Christian terminology, we will use that. Let us keep in mind here, too, that all is one—one First Cause, one God—the three aspects are one, but we have separated them to help us understand.

Manifestation begins with the Third Aspect—the Holy Spirit—the divine creative power, energy, or in-

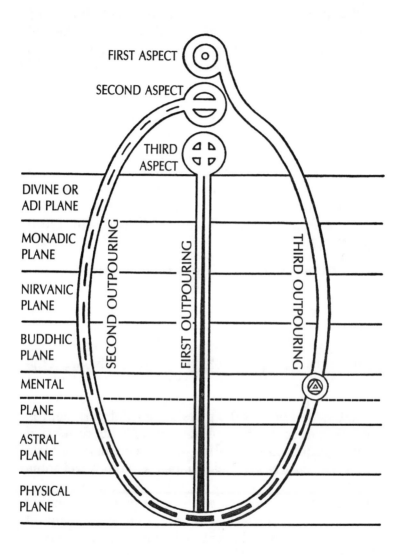

telligence. We find a reference to its activity in the Bible: "And the Spirit of God moved on the face of the waters." This is the aspect of God which creates matter, the atoms, at all levels, thus preparing the field in which all manifestation is to take place. It creates atoms and holds them together in molecules or elements, which become ever denser and denser as the energy is slowed down to lower and lower rates of vibration. At last it is so slowed down, so crystallized, that it appears to us as physical matter—dense, so-called solid matter. Modern physicists now tell us that matter is energy. They don't quite say "God's energy slowed down," but they have at least discovered it is energy.

The Evolution of Life and Consciousness

When the field of manifestation has been created, or prepared, the Second Aspect, the God the Son aspect, which is life or consciousness, takes that matter with its atoms, builds it into forms, and ensouls the forms. It is impossible for us to conceive what the forms might be like at the higher levels of existence; certainly they would not be objective, concrete forms such as we know at the physical level, but rather the archetypes or abstractions, capable of being developed into infinite multiplicities—every conceivable form that we know as physical shapes. We might get some concept of this if we tried to think of the abstract idea of "tree"—an idea that would contain every tree that has ever been or ever might be—"treeness" we might say; or the abstract idea of "triangle," capable of containing within itself every conceivable triangle.

This Second Aspect—the God the Son aspect—begins as a divine spark or seed, with everything latent or germinal. The initial process in manifestation of

this aspect is a process of the life or consciousness—
the divine seed—involving itself in denser and denser
matter and forms before it can begin the long process
of evolving itself back up, out of matter.

Now some people may ask, "What is the purpose
of all this? If life is already divine, why go through
all of this in order to reach the divine again?" Perhaps
it is hardly our province to question the purposes of
the cosmos, but it may be helpful in understanding
this whole process to use the law of correspondences
described in chapter 1. Let us consider the acorn and
the oak tree, and let the oak tree correspond to the
divine—the whole or one—and the acorn correspond
to the divine spark or seed. Picture in your imagination a perfect oak tree, complete with acorns, which
are of course part of it. Now we could just leave it at
that and the acorns could remain as part of the perfect
tree. But what happens? The acorn drops from the oak
tree, descends into matter—the earth—gets itself
buried in dense matter for a period of time in order
that it may evolve out of matter again, to become itself
a perfect oak tree, complete with acorns capable of
producing other oak trees, which in their turn can
repeat the same process.

In manifestation, unconscious perfection first moves
to conscious imperfection (as the divine seed involves
itself in matter), and finally through evolution develops to self-conscious perfection. The life or consciousness begins, then, as a divine spark, and the first
process is involution into denser and denser forms until it finally involves itself in the densest physical
matter—the mineral kingdom. Consider what life must
be like in the mineral. In this densest of physical matter life is most limited or restricted because of the ger-

minal or seed-like nature of that life and because the
dense matter in which it is involved provides the most
rigid form. It takes an extreme outside stimulus to call
forth any response whatsoever from the sleeping life
within.

So what do we find going on at the mineral level?
Tremendous, devastating upheavals—earthquakes,
volcanic eruptions, extreme heat, extreme cold, unbelievable pressures, deluges producing violent
floods. This process of the evolution of life in the
mineral kingdom is depicted in one episode of Walt
Disney's film *Fantasia* showing the formation of the
universe. In his inimitable way he vividly portrays
these great upheavals, these ceaseless cataclysmic dis-
plays of nature's irresistible forces. Surely these must
call forth some faint response from the sleeping life
within the mineral. Eventually—and we must remember that we are speaking of a period of millions and
millions of years—the involved life does begin to respond, and the matter does begin to be a little more
plastic until we finally have what we might call the
"kings" of the mineral kingdom in the jewels and
crystals.

Certainly anyone who has ever studied crystallog-
raphy has been filled with awe and wonder by the
beauty, symmetry, and precise formations of crystals.
One great crystallographer, who had been illustrating
the process of the formation of crystals with pictures,
concluded his lecture with these words: "Atom is thus
added to atom, and molecule to molecule, not boister-
ously or fortuitously, but silently and symmetrical-
ly, and in accordance with laws more rigid than those
which guide a human builder when he places his

bricks and stones together. . . . It runs, as if alive, into the most beautiful symmetric forms.'' If we could sum up the experience gained by life in the mineral kingdom, we might say that it learns to respond to outside stimuli and to build according to the laws of symmetry. The very rigidity of the matter in which it builds forces it to build according to the laws of symmetry.

There are no great leaps in nature, and scientists have difficulty drawing a fine line of demarcation between what can be classified as mineral crystal forms and some plant forms which seem to be almost mineral, as well as between some plant forms that seem to have characteristics of the animal kingdom. So the life that has evolved through the mineral kingdom moves on to begin experience in the plant kingdom. Now it is much more responsive to outside stimuli; plants being decidedly more sensitive than minerals. They still build according to the laws of symmetry but now in matter that is much more plastic, and we find the myriads of beautiful symmetric forms which make up the entire plant kingdom.

In addition, as the life moves on into the vegetable kingdom, it begins to develop that power of consciousness we call sensation, the ability to feel and react. In this kingdom we see responses to pleasure and pain, attraction and repulsion. Thus the life is gradually evolving or moving into the realms shown on the chart as the emotional plane. Plants will reach toward the things they like and withdraw from the things they do not like. Plants that like sun will turn in the direction of the sun; those that like water send their roots out in the direction of water. Those that do not like salt will withdraw their roots from the ground where salt has been sprinkled and send them out in the opposite direction. We may not be able to say that plants actually have emotions or feelings, but certainly there are indications that the consciousness in them is evolving through matter in that direction. Finally we come to what we might call the kings of the plant kingdom in the great majestic trees and beautiful flowers, and again the life or consciousness graduates from this kingdom and moves on for experience to the animal kingdom.

In the animal kingdom we find still greater response to outside stimuli; life continues to build according to the laws of symmetry, and the consciousness of sensation and pleasure and pain is much more highly developed. In fact animals run the gamut of all the lower emotions, and when we get to our most highly evolved domestic animals—those which we might think of as the "kings" of the animal kingdom, such as highly bred horses, dogs, or cats—we find at least an attempt at thought. People argue about whether animals actually think, but those who have had intelligent pets know that they make great attempts at times and try their very best to understand what you say or do for them. At least we see a reaching up toward the level of mind, shown on our chart as the mental plane.

The next point is a step which is often misunderstood. When we try to express this great scheme of life evolving through all the forms of nature in the vast sweep of evolution, people sometimes say, "You are trying to tell me I have been an animal," or they ask, "If I don't live this life as I should, will I come back as a butterfly or worm or something of the sort?" Now if you will follow the next step closely you will see that such a thing is just as impossible as it would be for the hen to become the egg again.

The Evolution of Spirit

Up to this point in evolution, the summit of the animal kingdom, we have only two aspects of God's nature in manifestation—the divine creative energy or Holy Spirit aspect, which has created matter, and the life or consciousness, God the Son aspect, which has taken that matter and built it into forms it has ensouled, first in the mineral, then in the plant, and finally in the animal kingdoms. It first involved itself in matter and then evolved up through matter to the point of reaching toward mind, where the triangle is placed on our diagram, and that is as far as it can go. Then, as if sensing its own incompleteness, it reaches up for fulfilment, for something more to be added. We sometimes see this happen when animals make great sacrifices or perform acts of heroism, love, and devotion, when a dog, for example, gives everything for its master in some supreme effort, as if reaching up to something higher, sacrificing the lesser to the greater.

The life thus reaching up, forms, as it were, a chalice into which, in response to this great upsurge, the God the Father aspect—pure spirit, uninvolved in matter in any way whatever—flashes down, and a human soul is created. This individualization process has been compared to a carbon arc lamp, with one positive pole and one negative. When the two are near enough to each other, the resistance of the air is overcome, the current jumps from one pole to the other, the arc is formed and the light blazes. Now we have pure spirit—which is divine will, divine love, and divine intelligence—added to these other two aspects of God that have been manifesting up to this point. Then and only then is a human soul created.

This new-born soul now has latent within it all the divine qualities, however germinal or seed-like. It is a God in the becoming. This evolutionary process continues through human evolution and on to super-human levels and on and on to levels beyond our capacity to comprehend until complete perfection is reached.

Solving The Three Mysteries

In the first chapter we mentioned three great gaps in the scheme of evolution as painted by science. A possible solution to those gaps, or mysteries, can be seen in the diagram. The first gap was the unanswered question, "Where does matter come from? How do the atoms or subatomic particles that start the creation of a universe arise?" The Third Aspect, the Holy Spirit or divine, creative energy aspect of God's nature, brings into being the necessary matter, shown as the central column of the diagram. The second gap was the unanswered question, "Where does the consciousness of living things come from? What about the first living cell?" Conscious life comes from the God the Son aspect which ensouls all forms and is represented by the left descending curve and its rise to the triangle on the chart. The third unanswered question was "Where does the first human come from, how does self-conscious humanity originate in this evolutionary process of science?" The human soul or individual is created only after the response of the God the Father aspect—pure spirit—has been added, which is represented by the meeting of forces at the triangle at the lower right of the diagram.

From Perspective to Adventure

Now, how does this larger framework of Theosophy—this viewing of life from the mountain top in its true perspective—this seeing all of life through the eyes of the real Self—change our attitude or approach to living? It can be revolutionary in its effect. It is like changing our center of awareness from the circumference or periphery of the wheel to the hub or center.

First of all, those with such a viewpoint realize that there is a supreme power, which is all-wise and all-loving, directing the universe; that there is a divine plan which is evolution or growth and progress for all life; that that plan is working for good regardless of the apparent chaos on the surface; and that the final attainment will be unimaginable glory for every human being. They know that they are part of that divine life and plan—that there is nothing else outside of God—with all capacity latent within themselves waiting to be unfolded. They know for a fact that all life is one great brotherhood. For them brotherhood is not sentimental nonsense or an impractical ideal; it is a reality and only that which is good for the whole can be really good for any single individual. They therefore cease selfish effort for personal gain and devote their lives to the service of all.

Next, they realize that the life of the true Self is the only life worth living, and they devote all their energies to that life. They cease to identify themselves with their bodies—their masks—and therefore gradually gain control of those bodies, which become perfect channels for expressing the divine life within. They regard all troubles or problems, all so-called evils, simply as outside stimuli, the resisting force which helps to call the true Self into full bloom and develop all of their latent capacities. They know that whatever comes to them is for their own good, regardless of how much their personality may feel otherwise, that there is no such thing as chance. They are aware that they are in the exact circumstances they have created to provide the means or opportunity by which they may take the next step forward, so they use them instead of longing for different circumstances.

They know death as a recurring and natural event in growth and so have no fear of such an event but discard the worn-out body much as they would a worn-out coat. They look on one lifetime simply as one day in the world school in which they learn the lessons of human evolution, and they try to apply themselves and learn their lessons well so that they may pass on and graduate and be more helpful to others. They know that they wake up each morning with the same capacities with which they went to bed, that no miracle happens overnight to change them from a third-grader to an eighth-grader, and that neither will they wake up tomorrow or begin their new incarnation with primitive abilities. They have developed the capacities of a great soul.

For such a vantage point all of life becomes a great adventure, a great drama in which we each have a part to play, a great symphony which will be completed only when we sound forth our own individual note in perfection to complete the one perfect harmony. Then will we truly know our real Self which is divine and our true destiny which is the attainment of Absolute Bliss.

For Further Reading:

From Atoms to Kosmos, by L. Gordon Plummer
Cosmic Evolution, by Adam Warcup
Man, God and the Universe, by I. K. Taimni
Theatre of the Mind, by Henryk Skolimowski

5

Reincarnation: An Ancient and Modern Idea

From time to time, in the growth of the civilization of the West, a great new idea dawns on human understanding. As this master concept is grasped, first by one person, then by a few, then by more and more, with it comes a greatly increased understanding of the nature of the objective forms of the universe which surround us, and of the subjective nature and significance of humanity in relation to these forms.

One such master concept, for example, which first dawned on the understanding of Westerners several hundred years ago, was the idea that the earth on which we live is not flat but round. As this idea was grasped, first by a few, then by more and more, until finally it came to be generally accepted, with it came a clearer objective picture of the nature of this Earth on which we live, then of its position in the solar system and the universe.

Another such idea which dawned on our Western understanding in the last century was the master concept of evolution, the great theory which shows that there is a scheme which links together the forms of all living things found on earth today or which ever have lived. This concept places every plant and creature somewhere on the main trunk, or on one of the branches of this ever-unfolding tree of evolution. As this idea was grasped, people saw the relationship of the objective forms of all living things to each other and something of their own relationship to them.

A third such idea, which is emerging in the understanding of the occidental world today, is the idea of reincarnation, which shows the human being as a pilgrim soul, moving forward rhythmically, over vast periods of time, to the unfoldment of spiritual powers. As we grasp this master concept, we gain a vastly increased understanding of the objective nature and position of humanity in this world of form, and of our subjective and spiritual relation to matter.

A strange thing about these ideas is that they were all known in the ancient cultures and had spread into the Mediterranean civilizations, which were the advance guard of modern Western culture. They were swept aside and lost after the fall of the Roman Empire. Very slowly at first, and then more rapidly, we have rediscovered them now in a form unencumbered by the encrustations of superstition and time which in older cultures had degraded or sometimes almost completely buried them.

A very natural reaction, and perhaps a purifying force, has been the opposition which has greeted these ideas as they have been presented by their champions. This opposition is natural, for these concepts fundamentally change our views on life and upset widely accepted ideas. The opposition to the idea that the earth is round was at first very strong, but it has gradually crumbled and has now almost disappeared.

Remnants of the old way of thinking still linger, however, and are championed by a small group of people who call themselves the *Flat Earthists* and insist that the earth is flat. The idea of evolution is more recent, and so the opposition to it, though steadily diminishing, is still quite strong and is represented by a considerable group of "creationists," who maintain that every living thing was spontaneously created as it is now by God as described in the Book of Genesis. The idea of reincarnation is still accepted by only a minority of the Western world, and the opposition largely confines itself to ridicule; but the concept is gaining adherents at an ever-increasing pace.

Schopenhauer said that when a new truth is presented to the world it passes through three phases. First, it is met with scorn and ridicule. Second, it is violently and forcefully attacked. Finally, it is accepted as a self-evident truth. These three stages may perhaps be seen in the reaction to the three ideas of the roundness of the earth, evolution, and reincarnation.

One of the great battle cries of the opponents of these master concepts has always been that they are unspiritual, that they degrade and belittle humanity. This opposition comes from a misunderstanding of their true nature for, when rightly understood, they cause human beings to stand in awe before the majesty and vastness of the laws which they reveal as governing the universe.

One of the greatest contributions of the Ancient Wisdom is to present reincarnation as the great spiritual idea which it is, proclaiming it as a new master concept in the West and reproclaiming its spiritual significance in the Orient. Reincarnation is here presented as the majestic method by which the divine spark in each human being moves steadily forward toward the expression of its divine nature in the world of form. It is presented unencumbered by superstition such as that which speaks of human beings reincarnating as animals or plants. Such changes are impossible as it is impossible for a hen to become an egg again.

One of the simplest methods of explaining reincarnation is by answering the questions which might be asked by a person meeting the idea for the first time. This method will be used here and in the following chapter to answer the following questions:

1. What is reincarnation?
2. What reincarnates?
3. Who believes in reincarnation?
4. Is reincarnation a Christian teaching?
5. What is the evidence for reincarnation?
6. Why do we not remember our past lives?
7. How does a belief in reincarnation affect our outlook on life?

What is Reincarnation?

The first question an inquirer might ask is "What is reincarnation?" By one definition, *reincarnation is the vast rhythmic process by which the spiritual self in a human being unfolds its spiritual powers in the world of form.* This process takes vast periods of time, commensurate with the periods of time which science sees as necessary for the evolution of the forms of living things.

Rhythmic motion seems to be a basic property of matter and of all living things. There are characteristic rhythms or vibrations of every chemical element by which we can identify it in the light of stars. There are the rhythms of sound waves, heartbeats, breathing; the rhythm of day and night and the human rhythm of waking and sleeping, which keeps pace with it. There are rhythms of the phases of the moon, of the seasons, vaster rhythms of ice ages followed by temperate periods, the majestic rhythm of the precession of the equinoxes, which require 25,000 years for one complete rhythmic swing. And, vastest of all science's rhythmic concepts, there is the idea that we may live in a "pulsating universe" where one complete cycle, or pulsation, will take several thousands of millions of years.

Reincarnation is one of the greater rhythmic processes of which one lifetime is but part of one pulsation. In the complete life cycle of a normal human being, we see the lowest part of one such vast pulsation of expression and withdrawal. Life begins by manifesting feebly through the infant body, quite unable to control its environment. Through childhood and youth, this life learns to use its instruments and to express itself more effectively while rushing forth for new experiences, eager to try everything and to conquer the world. It then passes on through maturity and gradually becomes more reflective and contemplative as it approaches old age. The desire for exciting new experiences fades, and the withdrawal of life is complete at death.

Many thinkers considering the forthgoing and return phases of human life have thought them to be the lower portion of a far greater rhythmic motion. The first phase is the descent of the soul, from its sublime, free, spiritual realms, to inhabit a baby form and to learn to express itself through that form. The second phase begins somewhere around the middle of life and continues after death in a process of withdrawal from the physical plane and assimilation, at successively higher levels, of the experiences on earth. Finally, having completely withdrawn and cast off all instruments of personal experience, it stands again in its spiritual and formless nature, ready to begin its next rhythmic manifestation and to descend into matter and to unfold more powers.

From such a viewpoint, which covers vast periods of time, what we call a lifetime is as a day in the life of the truly spiritual "I," who moves forward on a vast pilgrimage to the complete unfoldment of spiritual powers, every lifetime bringing that "I" closer to the great goal of complete self-expression.

During much of Western history, people's concept of time was limited to a few thousand years at most. Science broke this limitation for the physical world of nature, and the concept of reincarnation similarly breaks it for human life, showing us as immortal beings moving rhythmically forward in vast eras of time.

An analogy which some people have found helpful in trying to understand reincarnation is to compare the human soul to an eagle, perched in its aerie high above a lake. From time to time the eagle leaves its nest, dives into the lake, catches a fish, and returns to its nest where it eats, digests and assimilates the fish, and, after some time, once again becomes hungry and dives into the water for more food. This descent into the water corresponds to the soul's taking of a human body. Catching the fish may be compared to the gathering of experience in the world of flesh, and the time of digestion and assimilation to the time of digesting and assimilating of experiences during the periods between lives.

Of course analogies must not be carried too far; this one does however help in answering the question "How long is the period between lives?" The periods between the descents of the eagle depend in a general way on the size of the fish caught, and the periods between the descent of the soul into incarnation depend in a general way on the amount of experience gathered. However, a short life can be very rich in deep and significant experiences and a long life can run smoothly with few deeply stirring events. Also, the individual may still be unable to understand deeply and to assimilate experiences and thus to learn their lessons fully. In general however, a longer life would be followed by a longer period between lives; and a person with a spiritual and philanthropic outlook on life and its deeper meanings would pass a far longer period absorbing experiences between lives than would a simpler person living in a primitive society. The periods seem to range from a few years to several thousand years or even more in exceptional cases.

What Reincarnates?

The question "What reincarnates?" is perhaps one of the most difficult to answer, for in our language we have words for all the phenomena of matter, space, and time, but that which reincarnates is the part of man which belongs to the formless nonmaterial and timeless worlds. It is probably the impossibility of answering this question objectively which has led to the development of the idea that only the qualities of an individual reincarnate, not the actual individual. The physical body and all of its characteristics of height, strength, and complexion will not reincarnate. The emotional nature, with all its personal likes and dislikes, will not reincarnate. The mental nature, with its accumulated knowledge and its habits of thinking, will not reincarnate. That which is above all these aspects of the personality is what reincarnates.

In normal daily life we are not aware of this inmost self, "the Inner Ruler Immortal." In our moments of great inspiration, however, we transcend the limitations of form and time to a certain extent and feel the wonder and beauty of the life behind all forms around us. In these moments we are aware of our inmost Self, and we then know that which reincarnates.

The word *body* comes from an old Anglo-Saxon word *bodig* which means a dwelling place. The word *abode* also comes from the same root. This is what our bodies really are—the temporary abode or abiding place of the immortal Self which reincarnates.

In *The Idyll of the White Lotus*, Mabel Collins writes that the future of the reincarnating immortal Self "is the future of a thing whose growth and splendor has no limits."

Who Believes in Reincarnation?

People who ask the question, "Who believes in reincarnation?" are sometimes startled to be told that most people believe in reincarnation. It is undoubtedly true that if all human beings were questioned on their belief, most would assert belief in a great rhythmic process in which the spiritual self in us descends into incarnation again and again. There would be great differences of mass opinion in different areas and among different cultural and religious groups, the idea being very widely accepted in India and many oriental countries but by only a minority in Europe and America. The anthropologist Margaret Mead quoted a London *Sunday Times* poll about 1940 as showing that in England one person in eight, or about 12.5 percent, believed in reincarnation. The idea is becoming more and more generally accepted in Europe and America. A few years ago, Gallup polls showed that about 25 percent of Americans believe in reincarnation.

In addition to statistics, however, people who ask this question usually want to know the names of people whose opinions are respected and who have openly stated their belief in this great principle of rhythmic growth of an immortal Self by repeated descent into incarnation. Here then is a very brief and incomplete list to indicate the variety of people who hold such a belief:

Ralph Waldo Emerson	Kahlil Gibran
Oliver Wendell Holmes	Robert Browning
Alfred Lord Tennyson	Plato
Henry Wadsworth Longfellow	John Masefield
Johann Wolfgang von Goethe	William Wordsworth
Pythagoras	Arthur Schopenhauer
Walt Whitman	Shri Krishna
Gautama Buddha	Shirley Maclaine

A listener once commented that this list was composed entirely of artists, philosophers, poets, and religious leaders, and that practical people do not believe in reincarnation. Here are the names of a few practical people who have stated their belief in it:

Henry Ford	Lord Hugh Dowding
Thomas Edison	Benjamin Franklin
Napoleon Bonaparte	General George Patton

Benjamin Franklin lived at a time when the idea was almost unknown in America and would have been considered shocking by most people, yet he had a delightful way of stating new ideas in a whimsical, humorous manner—so amusing that they raised no objection. Here is his epitaph, proclaiming his belief in rebirth. It is inscribed on a brass plate beside his grave in Philadelphia:

> The body of Benjamin Franklin, printer, like the cover of an old book, its contents torn out and stripped of its lettering and gilding, lies here, food for worms.
>
> But the work shall not be lost, for it will, as he believed, appear once more in a new and more elegant edition, revised and corrected by the author.

Is Reincarnation a Christian Teaching?

Most Christian churches do not yet openly preach a belief in reincarnation, although there are many clergymen of different denominations who firmly believe in it. But it was a current belief among many of the peoples of Palestine at the time of the Christ. There are several references in the Bible to the general acceptance of this idea.

There is, for example, the well-known instance in which the Christ asked his disciples the question: "Whom do men say that I am?" The answers show that the question was understood to mean "Of whom do the people think I am a reincarnation?" for they said, "Some say John the Baptist; but some say Elias and other, Jeremiah, or one of the prophets" (Matthew 16:13-14). One unmistakable reference, in the words of the Christ himself, is his statement with regard to John the Baptist: "If ye will receive it, this is Elias which was for to come" (Matthew 11:14). Reincarnation gradually dropped from the outer teaching of the early Christian church although fragments of it appear in the doctrine of the Resurrection.

The idea of the resurrection of the bodies of all human beings is obviously a scientific impossibility, even if all the atoms in one person's body could be brought together again. Unquestionably many of the atoms used in a body have been used again in those of others, and all bodies could not therefore be resurrected simultaneously. The idea of the resurrection "of the body" may well be the result of interpretation and translation by those who failed to see the true meaning of the phrase. Perhaps it should be rendered as the resurrection "in a body." In spite of the fact that reincarnation is not one of the accepted teachings of the Christian church today there is a steadily increasing number of the clergy as well as the laity who believe in it and a smaller, and also steadily growing number, who preach the spiritual ideal of reincarnation.

For Further Reading:

Reincarnation: A New Horizon, by Sylvia Cranston
    and Carey Williams
Reincarnation Explored, by John Algeo
Reincarnation for the Christian, by Quincy Howe, Jr.
The World Within, by Gina Cerminara

6

Reincarnation: Rational Basis For Hope

In the last chapter, we looked at what reincarnation is and who believes in it. It is not enough, however, merely to know about reincarnation and to recognize that it is both an ancient and a modern belief. We must also consider why so many people have believed in it, and still do. We must look at evidence for and against it, and we must consider what effect an acceptance of the concept can have on our lives.

What is the Evidence for Reincarnation?

When inquirers ask for evidence of reincarnation, they usually first ask for the evidence of individuals who can remember past lives clearly and in detail. Ian Stevenson of the University of Virginia, a psychiatrist, has researched many such instances. His documentation of case histories of persons, especially children, who claim to remember previous lives is perhaps the best scientific evidence for reincarnation, though they seem to represent exceptional cases of rapid rebirth. However, Stevenson does not maintain that his cases prove reincarnation, only that they are suggestive of it.

Another kind of evidence is to be found in the reports of clairvoyants, people able to see worlds more ethereal than the physical, many of whom have investigated life after death and between-life states. Reports of this kind can be found in the writings of C. W. Leadbeater and others. Such evidence depends on the investigators' ability to observe accurately without unconsciously projecting their preconceptions and prejudices, which is difficult to do even in observing physical objects and events. Each inquirer must decide how much credence to put in these observers' statements, and so such evidence will not be considered here.

The next type of evidence, which periodically arouses much popular interest, is that of the statements of a subject in hypnotic trance, who is made to recall successively the events of youth, childhood, and infancy. An effort is then made to have the subject transcend the barrier of death and recall previous lives. An account of such an attempt, which created much interest, was published in the book *The Search for Bridey Murphy*. But this evidence is unsatisfactory also, for even if a person like the subject of this book described what she called her previous life, and subsequent investigations showed that the individual described had really lived and details were correctly given, and even if it was found impossible that she could have read or been told about that individual's life, the matter would still not be proved. Other possible explanations for such phenomena may be advanced by the skeptic: telepathy, clairvoyance, influence of a deceased spirit. J. B. Rhine, of Duke University, one of the outstanding authorities on the scientific evaluation of objective evidence in support of facts relating to nonmaterial phenomena, stated emphatically that such evidence would not be at all acceptable as scientific proof of reincarnation.

Where, then, are we to seek for evidence of reincarnation? We should proceed as scientists proceed when seeking the principle underlying a set of phenomena. They first observe as many examples of the phenomena as they can. Then they think over these examples and take as a hypothesis or possible explanation, some idea which may explain them all. Then they try to apply this to all their observations. If it does not fit, they discard it. If it fits and appears to apply in all cases, they will become more sure of its truth and may begin to call it a theory; and finally, after very widespread corroboration, they may announce it as a law.

Individuals considering the idea of reincarnation should first take it as a hypothesis and try to apply it to human life. They will then be able to decide whether, in their understanding of life, reincarnation should be accepted as a theory, or a law, or whether it should be discarded as not fitting the observed facts. They should not make the mistake of rejecting the obvious influences on human character such as heredity, environment, and psychological blocks, but neither should they assume that such influences explain all. The efforts to account for human capacity and behavior by these factors alone sometimes lead to the most solemn pronouncements of explanations which strain human credulity to the limit.

Let us then consider some phenomena, such as we meet in our everyday world, and see how simple and logical is their explanation when reincarnation is taken as a hypothesis and considered in addition to

the factors of heredity, environment, and psychological disturbances.

First, from time to time, child prodigies such as
Mozart appear. At the age of six Mozart was able to
play so beautifully that he toured Europe, charming
his listeners in all the courts. He was already a com-
poser at the same early age. How did a child gain the
capacity to put such beauty and depth of feeling into
his music, a capacity which many adults have failed
to achieve after a lifetime of study? The explanation
of reincarnation is that here is one who, in his previous
life or lives, had worked at the task of making music
a channel for the expression of beauty and truth. In
this life he had a musical heredity and a musical environment from birth, and he was probably reborn
very rapidly after his previous incarnation. Thus he
found in this life a clear channel through which this
capacity re-expressed itself immediately.

Such outstanding prodigies are rare and we seldom
meet them in daily life. But in any group of children
you will find that each has a certain aptitude or natural
capacity for some line of activity and little or no aptitude in other areas. The explanation of reincarnation
is that these natural capacities are the results of work
and training in previous lives, and the skills for which
an individual must now work so hard are those on
which little effort has been spent in the past. The limitations of physical heredity, environmental pressure,
and psychological strains must be recognized as real
factors, but they do not begin to give a full explanation of individual differences for many thinking
people.

All evidence for reincarnation depends ultimately
on memory, although the facts are not always recog-

nized as memory. What we have considered here is the memory of capacity or skill.

Let us now consider our relations with people around us. In our daily lives many of us meet hundreds of people, and with most of these the contact is purely superficial. Perhaps once in a lifetime, or even more often, we meet someone with whom we feel completely at ease immediately and with whom there is a deep mutual rapport. With that person we know that we can talk of the ideas and thoughts closest to our inmost nature and be assured of understanding. After discounting such factors as the attraction of the opposite sex and the fascination of a pleasing personality, reincarnation suggests that we are meeting again someone whom we have known, perhaps many times and in various relationships, in previous lives. Though we have never before met in this life, yet soul instantly recognizes soul and the understanding from that level pervades the personality. Such experiences, for those fortunate enough to have them, are striking corroboration of the hypothesis of reincarnation, through recognition of friends from the past.

Personal memories afford another area to which we can apply the hypothesis of reincarnation. Very few people can remember even isolated scenes from another incarnation; even fewer can review at will any or all of their previous lives, although this capacity will one day unfold in all of us. Many people, however, with no clairvoyant faculties whatever have vague and nebulous impressions of previous lives, which are, nevertheless, memories. These express themselves in a vague interest and a feeling of familiarity toward a certain nation, a certain religion, or a certain period of history. Perhaps the art work, the sculpture, or the ruins of some nation seem strangely familiar and fascinating. Some of these impressions, after the similarity with earlier environments has been discounted, are explainable only by reincarnation, as the vague and blurred memories of experiences among these things in previous lives.

Another kind of memory of experiences is that of the emotional impact of events in a previous life which made a deep impression—difficulties which, in that life, were never overcome. Such memories are frequently awakened by events in this life which have elements of similarity. For example, the horror and despair which resulted from being imprisoned in a previous life may be reawakened by a childhood experience of being shut up in a dark place. Perhaps only the emotions of fear and despair are recalled, while the details of the terrible experience which originally caused them are forgotten. These deep, painful emotions may then exert a crippling influence on the personality in this life. This is frequently the case in unexplainable fears such as fear of water, fear of heights, fear of the noise of an airplane motor, or fear of explosions and noises, which may recall disasters in previous lives caused by drowning, falls, crashes, or death on a battlefield.

Psychiatrists and others who trace back emotional blocks to outwardly insignificant events of childhood often get only to the outer circumstances of this life which reawakened the deep emotions connected with those major experiences of previous lives. But this discovery is important to the psychiatrist, who then works, quite correctly, on healing the emotional disturbance associated with such events. These are some of the verifications of reincarnation from our memories of previous events and places.

As we progress toward the unfoldment of the powers of the spiritual Self in the world of form, we have to unfold those virtues which we associate with noble people, such as courage, strength, mental power, patience, gentleness, and compassion. The perfect man or woman has all of these unfolded to the full. As we progress toward this goal, it may well happen that we will have a series of lives in one sex and then transfer to the opposite sex. The first life after the change is apt to be difficult, one in which we appear in the unfortunate role of the effeminate man or the masculine woman. There are other reasons for this phenomenon, but the hypothesis of reincarnation here gives a valuable key and shows why such individuals need our understanding.

The harmonious relationship between the majestic rhythm of reincarnation and the absolute certainty of natural law shows a magnificent scheme unfolding with perfect justice for every individual. This moral and ethical vindication of reincarnation is a most important piece of evidence, but it will not be discussed here as it is fully developed in the next chapter.

Here then are some of the factors to be considered by thoughtful persons who are willing to take reincarnation as a hypothesis and apply it, together with the facts of heredity, environment, and psychological disturbances, to the circumstances of life around them. They will then be able to decide for themselves if reincarnation is a reasonable hypothesis.

Why Do We Not Remember Our Past Lives?

The questioner who asks "Why do we not remember our past lives?"is under a misapprehension, for unquestionably the real Self, that which reincarnates, *does* remember. However, the questioner usually means "Why do we not remember the details of previous lives such as names and physical appearances, occupations and adventures, home life and family relationships?"

In order to answer this question, let us first see what we remember and what we forget of our present incarnation. Most of us have learned to read and write in this life. We probably acquired these skills by attending classes in primary school for some years. If today we were asked to describe in detail the lesson on a specific day, most of us would be unable to answer such simple questions as: "Who was the teacher?" "What was the lesson you learned and who were the other students in the class?" We have forgotten this mass of unimportant detail connected with the learning, but we remember the essence of those many experiences and use it whenever we read and write. So it is with memory of past lives. The details of experiences in previous lives are forgotten, but we carry with us, and use constantly, the essence of those experiences.

In previous lives we have all made decisions and performed actions of far-reaching consequence, bringing sorrow or happiness in their wake. The details of those decisions and consequences are all forgotten, but their essence is remembered and guides and directs us in this life when we have similar problems to face, similar decisions to make. It speaks to us as "the still small voice," the voice of conscience, which is the memory of our past experiences. The existence of individual conscience helps to explain why some people, even though they have been taught otherwise by parents, at school, and by religious teachers, will commit robbery if they can get another person at a disadvantage and think they can avoid capture. Others, who sometimes have had little moral instruction in this life, nevertheless feel, in their inmost being, that such action is wrong and will have none of it.

There is considerable evidence that we do in fact remember. As has been said, there are the memories of skills and accomplishments which express themselves in *natural aptitudes* in this life. Then there are the memories of individuals occasionally expressing themselves in sudden and deep *friendships;* memories appearing as *fascination* for certain countries, cultures, and art work; memories showing themselves as *unreasonable fears,* and the memory we sometimes call *conscience.* In such ways as these we do remember our previous lives.

How Does a Belief in Reincarnation Affect Our Outlook on Life?

One who believes in reincarnation realizes that the body and personality, which are usually mistaken for the self, form only the temporary outer husk of the real self, the soul within. From this point of view it is wrong to say, "I have a soul," if by "I" we mean the outer form of flesh and blood and the personality that goes with it, for these are temporary things which will disintegrate at the end of the earthly life. Such a mortal creature cannot possess something which is immortal and spiritual. The statement should be reversed. It should be said, "I *am* a soul and *have* a body." We have bodies for the period of a lifetime and then discard them as we discard worn-out clothes. Looked at from this point of view, things such as prestige, power, wealth, and fame, which we gain or lose for one lifetime only, are relatively insignificant.

The significant things are the qualities we are building into our immortal characters, the future opportunities we are preparing by our actions, and the human links of all kinds which we are making that will determine our future contacts. This outlook gives believers in reincarnation a completely different standard by which to judge themselves and others, to evaluate events, and to plan actions.

When those with an understanding of reincarnation see a child, they know that they are seeing one whose mind is not like a blank slate, on which teachers and parents can write what character and capacities they choose. They know that they are looking at the instrument of a soul who is seeking to express, more fully, capacities already partly developed in the past and to develop new qualities and powers in this life. Parents and teachers have a great privilege and responsibility to train the new body and personality to be healthy, pure, and alert, to be self-controlled and free from fear. They can provide the healthy environment in which the shoots of future qualities and powers may develop into buds, which will later blossom forth as the expressions of the beauty of the soul within.

Such a believer sees all humanity as forming a great life wave, moving steadily forward to a magnificent goal. No matter how high or how low we may stand, we see some who are ahead of us from whom we can learn, some who stand at our own level with whom we can work side by side, and others behind us who need our help. Thus we learn the great law that progress for one can be made only by helping others. The individual who thus sees the great spiritual reality behind the law of reincarnation feels awe in contemplating the majesty of the steady forward movement of all humankind and is filled with reverence for the Great Law which controls and directs this stupendous scheme.

For Further Reading:

Cathars and Reincarnation, Arthur Guirdham
Experiencing Reincarnation, by James S. Perkins
Reincarnation, by Annie Besant
Reincarnation: Fact or Fallacy? by Geoffrey Hodson
Twenty Cases Suggestive of Reincarnation, by Ian Stevenson

7

A Question of Justice

There comes a time in the lives of nearly all of us when we begin to question the justice of life. Sometimes this questioning comes because of circumstances in which we find ourselves; sometimes because of something that has happened to those near and dear to us; sometimes because of apparent injustices which we see happening to the larger family of humanity. We cannot look anywhere about us without observing every kind of inequality, apparent injustice, and undeserved suffering, until it is no wonder many people begin to question whether there is a God at all and, if so, whether God is just.

Why are there so many apparently unearned gifts and opportunities and so much seemingly undeserved suffering? Why should one child be born in the slums, unwanted, unloved, surrounded by disease and poverty, with no opportunities, and another be born with loving and intelligent parents who provide every possible opportunity? Why is one particular child struck down and crippled for life by a careless driver? Did that innocent child do anything to deserve such a life of handicaps and suffering, or is it all just chance? Why was it *that* child instead of you or me? If there is justice in the world, why should some people be born with strong healthy bodies and others weak, diseased, deformed, handicapped, and sickly? Why are some endowed with great intellectual capacity and some born imbeciles? What has the newborn child done to deserve such heritage?

Natural Law

Turn where we will, the world is full of inequalities, apparent injustices, and moral chaos. And yet, while there seems to be no pervading law of justice governing our moral or intangible world, when we turn to the laws of nature and the physical world we find the complete opposite. Our entire modern material civilization rests on the dependability and immutability of natural law. Nature is synonymous with law. Fire does not burn today and freeze tomorrow.

Have you ever stopped to think how we depend on natural laws and what would happen if they suddenly ceased to work? Consider the laws of electricity. If you press the switch and the light does not go on, you do not ask if the laws governing the flow of electricity have suddenly changed; rather, you wonder what is wrong with the equipment, whether a fuse is blown or the power turned off; but you rely on the laws of electricity being unchanged. All of our modern manufacturing is made possible because of the dependability and immutability of the laws of chemistry and physics. The making of everything from a paper bag to a giant steel bridge is possible only because natural processes are predictable, controlled by immutable natural laws, laws which human beings have discovered and used.

Do we have to guess when we put an acorn in the ground whether we will get an apple tree, or a rose-bush, or an oak tree? The law is always the same; it always works, and for this reason we can learn the law and learn to use it. Our knowledge and understanding of nature's laws may change, but the laws themselves remain exact, dependable, and immutable whether we are considering astronomy and the laws that govern the heavens or the law of gravity as it affects our earth. They always work—we can always rely on them, and so we discover them and live in accordance with them.

One such law which is well known to every scientist is Newton's Third Law of Motion: "For every action there is an equal and opposite reaction." We understand this law in the physics laboratory, working with inorganic matter, because we can control the experiments there. However, until we study Theosophy, most of us do not realize that this law applies just as thoroughly to human beings—not only in our physical actions, but also at the emotional, mental, and moral levels of being. The law is just as exact, immutable, and dependable on these levels as it is on the physical. We can use it to create whatever kind of world we want for ourselves.

One reason for our inability to understand the application of this law of action and reaction to human existence is that we are not yet able to see enough of our pilgrimage through the human evolutionary process. We are unable to trace all of the effects we are experiencing at present back to their original causes. Nor can we follow all of our present actions through to the completion of their reactions in the future.

Sometimes the sequence of action and reaction is immediate and perceivable. If you put your hand in the fire you get burned and that is fairly immediate. Sometimes the reaction takes a longer period of time to occur. Suppose you neglect the laws of dental hygiene; it may take ten years before that reaction catches up with you and you have to suffer it out in the dentist's chair. Sometimes an even longer period of time is needed for it to become apparent that the law works. If the element of time is a factor, then as we limit our concept of time we shall increase the apparent inequalities and injustices in just the same proportion. Let us experiment a little with this element of time and see what happens.

A Day as a Lifetime

For a few moments, let us try in imagination to limit our world to a twenty-four-hour existence, instead of a lifetime of eighty or one hundred years, by which we ordinarily view and judge events. Remember now, we can know nothing of life except what we can observe in a twenty-four-hour period—we know nothing of yesterday's actions or tomorrow's reactions. What would we find? Would we see any further injustices or chaos?

Perhaps the first thing that would strike us would be the tremendous differences between human bodies. We may think they are unequal with our present concept of time but what would be our thoughts if we judged them on a twenty-four-hour basis? We would see little, weak, helpless bodies that had to be cared for and fed—had to have everything done for them and could do nothing in return but sleep or cry for more food and attention. We would see other bodies, big and strong and well-formed, capable and efficient, doing all the work and caring for these weak, helpless bodies.

What would be our reaction? Equality? Justice? Nothing could seem further from the truth with only a twenty-four-hour perspective on such a situation. "What," we might ask, "has this individual done to deserve a lifetime of struggle and helplessness in such a body?" We would have no way of knowing that this was a baby, that the parents had once been helpless babies and were cared for by other parents in turn, that the infant would, given time, grow into an independent, capable adult. We would simply see these completely unequal human beings and think how unjust it was and wonder how there could be a divine intelligence when such chaos existed.

Further, considering only those adults in the prime of life whose physical and mental capacities appeared more equal, what would we discover? Here also, we would find complete injustice, inequality, and chaos. One has been favored with a great gift—a skillful body that can produce beautiful music, while another, who appears to have the same kind of body, cannot play a note. "What," we would ask, "has this one done to earn such a gift, and that one to be deprived of it?" Certainly nothing as far as we could see. We would have no way of knowing that the musician had spent years of effort and energy studying and training that body to become musical and in youth had no more skill or ability than the other, who refused to study and practice.

From a twenty-four-hour perspective, what might we think of the individual suffering from the effects of an alcoholic spree the night before? How terrible! Through no fault of his own he has an entire life of suffering—his misery begins with the beginning of his life and lasts to the end. We would have no way of knowing what had gone on the night before to cause the suffering—neither would we have any way of knowing that tomorrow he probably would be completely recovered and a little wiser, perhaps, for the experience. All we would see would be a life of suffering, apparently entirely undeserved as far as his observable actions were concerned.

So we could go on in our imagination picturing many other situations that would make such a world unjust, unequal, and completely incomprehensible as far as the law of cause and effect or justice was concerned. Think of individuals having a "day off"—a complete life of leisure as far as we could see. Maybe that is the only day they ever had off and they work all the others, but we would not know this. Think of some individuals putting their money in the bank while others are spending, some planting crops while others are reaping a harvest, the student struggling in school while the professor seems to have been born with all the knowledge, and so on. Everywhere we would see complete injustice and chaos.

In our twenty-four-hour perspective, just as life would start when the sun came up and the day began, so all would end when the sun set and the world became cold and dark; everyone would go to sleep, all life and activity would cease, and that would be the end of existence. We would have no way of knowing that after a rest, the sun would rise again and the whole process would continue, that each would begin the next day exactly where he left off the night before, not only as far as worldly possessions and physical things were concerned, but with the same problems, dispositions, characteristics, and capacities—the same loves, the same hates, and the same hopes and fears. A person who had been a ditch-digger or bootblack would not wake up the following day a chemist or senator, neither would a great surgeon or artist awaken with merely the ability to sell newspapers.

It is easy enough for us to understand this twenty-four-hour cycle when we use our enlarged vision of a whole lifetime. In just the same way we need to expand our vision to include our entire human pilgrimage in order to understand this one lifetime. We begin this incarnation with exactly what we had of credits and debits at the end of the last life. Every strength or virtue of character which we build or unfold is ours for all time. We are the creators of our own destinies. "We are each our own absolute lawgiver, the dispenser of glory or gloom to ourselves." The chains that bind us are of our own forging, and we can file them away or rivet them more strongly.

Law as Opportunity

It is not a question of reward or punishment. The laws of nature are not commands which say we must do this or do that. They are simply statements of certain successions or sequences. Fire produces heat—that is the law. What we do with that law is our own affair—we can use that heat to keep us warm, heat our homes, or cook our food, or we can use it to destroy life and property. If one person plants flowers and another plants weeds, we do not blame God and say that the weeds are given as punishment. If we want flowers we must plant flowers. If a cook chooses ingredients and combines them to get porridge, we don't say God is unjust because the dish turns out to be porridge instead of pie. Maybe the cook wants porridge. But if we want pie all we have to do is combine the ingredients according to the laws of cookery and we will get pie.

If we want happiness all we have to do is sow the seeds of happiness according to natural laws which are just as exact and just as immutable as any other law of nature. "Nature is conquered by obedience." We learn through a study of Theosophy that nothing merely happens in moral law any more than in physical law—all are natural laws. But sometimes we need to expand our limited concept of time to find the causes of some of the present effects or circumstances and to recognize them as the opportunities they are.

The circumstances in which we find ourselves at the present time are the result of our past actions. As we give happiness or misery to others, so we reap in return—sometimes immediately and sometimes after longer lapses of time. Sometimes we have to look over many life-times in order to see the complete process.

Our present opportunities are the result of our past desires. The strongest force in the universe is the force of attraction and repulsion (the repulsion being, of course, just the negative aspect of this force). We should be very careful about what we desire. There is nothing more sure than that the people or things you really want or desire will be attracted to you through this force, although they may take a long time to reach you. Often, as time passes, we change our minds—we change our ideas of what we want or desire—and then we find ourselves tied to the result of our former desires. We must therefore be very careful what we long for; be sure it is what we really want.

Our present character is the result of our past thoughts. The one creative force in the whole universe is divine thought—divine creative intelligence—a fragment of which is in each one of us. Annie Besant, the reformer and second president of the Theosophical Society, said, "God's thought makes Universes; your thought makes yourself; it is the one creative force by which you shape, mould and build your character." If we do not like ourselves the way we are, the only thing that is ever going to change us is to change our thinking.

There is one other aspect we need to keep in mind as we study and try to understand this great law of justice. We are not only in the exact circumstances we ourselves have created, but we are also in the best possible place to unfold our next spiritual capacity. The law is entirely beneficent, regardless of how we may think otherwise at times. We can usually see this when we look back on situations and circumstances.

We are not here by chance. It is no accident that we happen to be here instead of in China or the South Sea Islands or somewhere else. When we learn our lesson, when we unfold that next capacity that circumstances and life are trying to teach us, when we take our next step forward, then we will find our circumstances have a miraculous way of changing. It is not the world that needs changing; it is ourselves. We make the world what it is by being what we are.

The wise person does not blame God, or neighbors or fate, but learns the laws of life and lives in accordance with them. For, as we are told in the Bible, "Be not deceived, God is not mocked, whatsoever a man soweth, that shall he also reap." We can sow whatever we will and be confident that it will grow and flower and come to fruit. And this law holds true not only in sowing seeds in the earth but also in sowing seeds in our minds and in our hearts.

For Further Reading:

Cayce, Karma and Reincarnation, by I. C. Sharma
The Christening of Karma, by Geddes MacGregor
Karma, by Annie Besant
Karma and Creativity, by Christopher Chapple
Karma: The Universal Law of Harmony, Ed. Virginia Hanson and Rosemary Stewart
Karma and Rebirth, by Christmas Humphries
Other Lives, Other Selves, by Roger J. Woolger

8
Our Inner Nature

We each create a little world of our own which surrounds us and colors and affects everything we see and do. We all know people, living in the most fortunate circumstances, who nevertheless surround themselves with a little world of gloom that darkens everything they see and tends to sadden or depress all who come near them. On the other hand, we all know people who have received many blows from fortune but who, nevertheless, surround themselves with a little world of sunshine that shows them the best in everything and brightens the world for all who enter their presence.

Clairvoyance

Theosophical literature has much helpful information about why our inner worlds differ and how we can make our worlds beautiful and joyous. Much of this information is obtained through senses more subtle than our well-known five. Today these faculties are called E.S.P. (extrasensory perception) or psychic powers. The word *clairvoyance*—literally "clear seeing"—which denotes the capacity to see worlds of matter subtler than the physical, is more specific. Because possession of these faculties is so frequently misunderstood, let us see where they belong in the plan of human unfoldment.

In the early stages of human evolution, man's consciousness was not fully implanted in the physical world. Even now, entities and forces of the invisible worlds are sometimes able to impress themselves on some individuals, to frighten them, delude them, or suggest ideas to them. Individuals who can be influenced in this way certainly possess a type of clairvoyance, but it is not under their control. It is the nonmaterial entity, not the individual, who is master. This type of clairvoyance is therefore called *negative clairvoyance* because it is the invisible agent that controls the medium, not the medium who controls the "invisible."

Negative clairvoyance is quite common. Many people who live in simple cultures have it; some animals have it; certain hereditary groups have it; many mediums, operators of ouija boards, fortune tellers, and others deliberately try to develop it. Such development often results in the individual's having less control, instead of more, over his own personality.

Human beings in general now stand at that stage in evolution where our consciousness is concentrated on the physical plane; we are learning to control and to use wisely the forces of the material world. While we are doing this we are only subconsciously influenced by the invisible worlds and their forces. Our civilization, and the human-made dangers and uglinesses which threaten and disgrace it, show how far we must develop before we can wisely and nobly use the forces of this physical world and be ready to handle the more wonderful, but also more dangerous, powers of the invisible worlds. It is therefore natural and right—indeed, a wise provision of nature—that people today should, in general, not have clairvoyant powers.

In the future, however, the time will come when we will have learned to use wisely, and for the service of our fellows, the tremendous powers of the physical world, such as atomic energy. When this stage is reached, we will begin once more to see and know of the existence of entities and forces in the invisible world. We will learn to use, not to be used by, nature's finer forces, and we will develop the kind of clear-seeing called *positive clairvoyance*.

Full, positive clairvoyance is extremely rare today, and those who possess it are always forceful, strong-willed people, who seldom mention, and never commercialize their powers. Their number will slowly increase.

Between the extremes of positive and negative clairvoyance are the enormous majority of today's psychics, mediums, and clairvoyants, who possess a mixture of the positive and negative faculties. Possession of clairvoyant powers is not of itself a mark of spirituality. One with clairvoyant powers may be wiser or more foolish, more spiritual or less so than one who has none.

It is well to remember that clairvoyance will develop in us all in nature's good time when we have built a strong character and a noble moral nature, and are leading an upright and spiritual life in the physical world. To try to unfold it prematurely by such artificial means as gazing at lights or mirrors, taking drugs, or practicing unnatural breathing rhythms, usually leads to negative clairvoyance, which is dangerous. There are no short cuts, no artificial means of developing spirituality, which is the only sure and natural way to develop positive clairvoyance. This does not mean that those who have the clairvoyant faculty should not use it. They should. Applying such tests of reality and accuracy as are used in science, they should seek to change it into ever more positive clairvoyance. But those who do not have it would do well to concentrate on the development of character, which is the only solid and natural basis for the later development of positive clairvoyance.

Personality and the Bodies

When studying our inner nature, remember that we are immortal spiritual beings who use a mortal personality for one lifetime only. After the death of the personality, the spiritual Self assimilates the essence of its life experiences. It then takes a fresh personality and seeks to express itself more fully through this new instrument. As it passes through many such incarnations, slowly the spiritual Self will learn more and more fully to show itself. Through the physical body it will manifest as grace, strength, and right action. It will shine through the emotions as friendliness, affection, compassion, reverence, and right feeling. Through the mind it will express itself as wisdom, understanding, and right thought.

Knowledge of the inner aspects of human nature is of value to one who seeks to mold the personality into an instrument for the expression of the will, love, and wisdom of the spirit within. Therefore, as each aspect of the inner nature is considered, its characteristics and habits are also discussed from the point of view of its likely reaction as we seek to mold it into harmony with the spiritual self. J. Krishnamurti's book *At the Feet of the Master* gives simple advice to one who seeks to do this. Therefore, in the following description, statements that summarize the findings of positive clairvoyants on the invisible aspects of the personality are followed by descriptions from that book of how these bodies, or aspects of our personalities, will behave and how they can be molded to express the spiritual Self. The accompanying diagram shows the three bodies through which the spiritual Self functions in the world as though they were on different levels, although in fact they all interpenetrate each other.

Spiritual Self ★

Mental -----------------------------

Emotional ----- (Astral)

Physical ------------   ------------

Dense Body and Etheric Double

The physical body has two aspects: that which is studied in anatomy and is composed of the solid, liquid and gaseous matter which we feel and use; and a subtler counterpart, not so sensed and not generally recognized today. This subtler aspect, composed of "etheric matter," is of shape and size similar to the dense physical body which we see, and for this reason it is called the *etheric double* or the *etheric counterpart*. It is faintly luminous, of a pale violet or lavender color, and has very little weight. This etheric double is essentially the life-containing or conserving aspect of the physical body.

The etheric double has three principal functions. First, it forms the mold or pattern into which the dense physical matter will grow during prenatal life and in recovering from wounds. It is therefore of great importance to infants and young people, and also to the healing of an injured body. Defects in the etheric double will produce defects and infirmities in the dense physical form.

Second, the etheric double assimilates and stores vitality from the sun and atmosphere and distributes it through the body as nervous energy. This can sometimes be seen as the "health aura" radiating in straight lines from the body of a healthy, vital individual, especially streaming from the tips of the fingers and toes. These lines tend to droop and weaken in a sick or nervously exhausted individual.

Third, the etheric double forms the link through which the consciousness of the spiritual self, descending through even subtler forms, finally reaches the dense physical body. This link, or bridge, can be made temporarily impassable to consciousness by a sudden shock or jarring of the physical body, such as a blow on the head which "knocks" the individual unconscious. A sudden emotional shock at the other end of the etheric bridge also can render it impassable to consciousness. This type of unconsciousness is called fainting. The etheric bridge also becomes impassable to consciousness under the influence of certain chemicals and drugs, such as chloroform, or through disturbances of the physical body, particularly if they affect the nervous system or the circulation of blood in the brain.

At death, the link between the physical and the higher bodies is permanently broken. The etheric double withdraws from the dense physical body and may perhaps float near that body for a few days, slowly disintegrating. It is sometimes seen as a wraith in graveyards. When a person in vigorous health dies suddenly, as in an accident or in war, the etheric double may automatically proceed to carry out the intention in the person's mind at the moment of death and may be seen by those with only slight clairvoyant faculties as a completely unintelligent, speechless ghost. In Shakespeare's *Macbeth*, the ghost of Banquo, murdered at Macbeth's order on his way to a feast, is the etheric double with no intelligence or power to speak. In his overwrought nervous condition, while thinking guiltily and intensely of Banquo, Macbeth has a temporary clairvoyant glimpse, and he alone sees the "ghost" at the feast. The ghosts and occult phenomena in Shakespeare's plays are depicted with an accuracy that only a great occultist would possess.

An outstanding characteristic of the matter of the physical world is its quality of inertia, its resistance to change and movement. It is, therefore, especially the *will* aspect of the spiritual nature which expresses itself and so develops through the physical body, in right and beautiful action and service.

In *At the Feet of the Master* the aspirant is given this advice with regard to the bodies:

But the body and the man are two, and the man's will is not always what the body wishes. When your body wishes something, stop and think whether *you* really wish it. For you are God, and you will only what God wills; but you must dig deep down into yourself to find the God within you, and listen to His voice, which is your voice. Do not mistake your bodies for yourself— neither the physical body, nor the astral, nor the mental. Each one of them will pretend to be the Self, in order to gain what it wants. But you must know them all, and know yourself as their master. . . . The body is your animal—the horse upon which you ride. Therefore you must treat it well, and take good care of it; you must not overwork it, you must feed it properly on pure food and drink only, and keep it strictly clean always, even from the minutest speck of dirt. For without out a perfectly clean and healthy body you cannot do the arduous work of preparation, you cannot bear its ceaseless strain. But it must always be you who control that body, not it that controls you.

The book goes on to describe how the physical body commonly responds:

When there is work that must be done, the physical body wants to rest, to go out walking, to eat and drink; and the man who does not know says to himself: "I want to do these things, and I must do them." But the man who knows says: "This that wants is *not* I, and it must wait awhile." Often when there is an opportunity to help some one, the body feels: "How much trouble it will be for me; let some one else do it." But the man replies to his body: "You shall not hinder me in doing good work."

Emotional Body

Beyond the dense and etheric levels of the physical world is a world of subtler matter which freely inter-penetrates and moves throughout the physical world. It is largely free of the physical limitation of inertia or "heaviness." Instead of will, muscle, and energy, it is emotion, desires, feelings which affect this mat-ter. It is therefore often called the *emotional world* or *plane*. Because of its self-luminous characteristic, it is also called the *astral world*. Colors are brilliant and constantly changing in response to surges of emotion. While few people consciously see these colors, it is surprising how many correct references to them have crept into the English language. A person who says, "I was so angry I saw red," is unconsciously recogniz-ing that anger surrounds its creator with a vivid, ugly red. Similarly, "She turned green with envy" or "He was in black despair" correctly refers to the unpleas-ant green and black which surround those express-ing such emotions. On the other hand, those who are full of good will and affection for all are surrounded by an aura of rose color, and to say "They look at the world through rose-colored glasses" is to describe the situation correctly. A beautiful blue is always associ-ated with devotion, and a lovely, soft green with sym-pathy and tenderness.

To function in the emotional or astral world, we have an *emotional* (or *astral*) *body*. It has a central part, of the same size and shape as the physical body, but it also has an outer part or aura, ovoid or egg-shaped in appearance, in which matter is much less concentrated than in the central body and constantly circulates, changing color and brilliance under the influence of our emotions.

When we sleep, our consciousness is released from its prison-house of the flesh. The emotional and subtler bodies withdraw from the physical, leaving it "asleep." There then lie great possibilities before us, for without the inertia of a physical body, almost unlimited travel is possible. If our emotional interests are of a coarse type, requiring a physical body for their expression and satisfaction, we will remain hovering near our sleeping physical body. But if we have wide esthetic and philanthropic interests and ties of affection beyond the physical, we may easily learn to travel and pursue these interests. Dreams of flying, or of being so light that one can jump over a house, a valley, or a landscape, or of walking in space, are often recollections of early experiences of this astral travel. We may visit loved ones in remote places, especially if there is cause for anxiety. Such "astral visitors" can often help in ways that are usually unrecognized and unremembered, although spectacular instances of dream recall and even of direct physical help are occasionally reported.

A characteristic of the emotional body is that it enjoys expressing violent passions of all kinds, and so those who wish to use it to express right feeling, to surround themselves with an atmosphere of serenity and good will to all, must learn to control it as a rider controls an excitable horse.

In *At the Feet of the Master* we read:

> The astral body has *its* desires—dozens of them; it wants you to be angry, to say sharp words, to feel jealous, to be greedy for money, to envy other people

their possessions, to yield yourself to depression. All these things it wants, and many more, not because it wishes to harm you, but because it likes violent vibrations, and likes to change them constantly. But you want none of these things, and therefore you must discriminate between your wants and your body's.

The idea of treating this body like an animal, and exercising but not overworking it, of giving it pure food and drink only and keeping it clean, is very helpful. If you deliberately send thoughts of affection and good will to one in need of help, you are exercising the emotional body in the right way and strengthening its power to serve you. If you spend a few moments each day reading a book which rouses beautiful emotions, you are feeding it on pure food and drink. If you turn it away from unpleasant, unclean emotions to those you wish it to express, you are keeping it clean.

Mental Body

Interpenetrating the emotional and physical worlds is a world of still finer matter, more self-luminous than the astral world. Thought is the driving force here and so it is called the *mental world*. As on the astral plane the physical limitation of inertia and weight is left behind, giving freedom in space and freedom from fatigue, so, in the mental world, further limitations lessen and fade. One of these is the necessity to use language to communicate. Time to some extent, although not completely, may also be transcended so that, as thoughts (the forerunners of all physical action) are seen, something of their future fruits and their roots in the past are simultaneously understood.

We have a *mental body* with which to function in this mental world. It has its central core, which is shaped like the physical body, and its mental aura. As the astral body changes with the fluctuations of the emotions, the mental body constantly changes under the influence of thought. In many people, the mental body is little vivified because they live far more in the astral world, seeking emotional excitement and new thrills for their pleasure, rather than exploring the world of thought.

In the early stages, this mental body grows by responding to every outside stimulus. In those who live on a bare subsistence level, it responds to the sound of a breaking twig on a jungle path, or a movement in the grass and indicates to the physical body a danger or a possible source of food. Thus a "grasshopper mind" is the natural, early development pattern for the mental body. Later development comes through concentration and the capacity to shut out all extraneous sounds and thoughts, to direct the entire power of the mental body to the subject under consideration. Many people can do this in moments of crisis only. The developed person does it habitually.

The mental body is the subtlest aspect of the personality and the last to unfold. Beyond (or within) the upper reaches of the mind, consciousness enters the realm of the immortal Self (called the Ego in much theosophical literature) where the unity of all life is known and the personality becomes aware of its oneness with all that lives. It seems that as the mind develops, the personality makes a last stand to maintain its former sense of self-separateness. The dewdrop resists slipping into the shining sea. The weaknesses of separation, pride, and selfishness may hold aspirants in a shell of aloof separation unless they control and direct the mental body.

In *At the Feet of the Master* it is said:

> Your mental body wishes to think itself proudly
> separate, to think much of itself and little of others.
> Even when you have turned it away from worldly
> things, it still tries to calculate for self, to make you
> think of your own progress, instead of thinking of the
> Master's work and of helping others. When you med-
> itate, it will try to make you think of the many different
> things which *it* wants instead of the one thing which
> *you* want. You are not this mind, but it is yours to use;
> so here again discrimination is necessary. You must
> watch unceasingly, or you will fail.

The same principles of exercise, of feeding on pure
food and drink only, and of cleanliness apply to the
mental body. Their corresponding meanings in the
mental world can be worked out by any thoughtful
person.

The Whole Personality

While we are physically awake, a portion of our consciousness is, so to speak, imprisoned in the physical
body. Even then, however, we are influenced by the
emotions and thoughts around us. For example, in a
crowd we may become so excited that we do things
we would never do without the stimulating emotional
atmosphere of the crowd. Under such circumstances,
some people "get religion" and "step up" for Jesus.
Others become part of a lynch mob.

In addition, we are unconsciously as well as consciously conditioned by the thought patterns of the
culture in which we live. We share the values and prejudices of our nation without examining them. We
assume that they are normal for everyone, whereas
they may be limited and parochial. Only very strong
individuals can feel and think for themselves in the

midst of emotional hysteria and firmly established thought patterns. Those few hear a different drummer and march to a different beat, as Thoreau said. They are the ones who influence others more than they are influenced.

Although the personality has been considered here in its three aspects of the physical, emotional, and mental bodies, yet it is a unit. Just as a student of physiology might study separately the nervous system, the muscular system, the digestive system, etc., while never forgetting that these different systems cannot exist independently of the entire body, so we study the characteristics of the physical, emotional, and mental bodies, while never forgetting that they are integral parts of the living personality.

For Further Reading

The Chakras, by C. W. Leadbeater
Clairvoyance, by C. W. Leadbeater
The Etheric Double, by A. E. Powell
Our Psychic Sense, by Phoebe Bendit and Laurence Bendit
This World and That, by Phoebe Bendit and Laurence Bendit

9
Life After Death

It seems extremely important to try to understand something about the process we call death because of the great amount of sorrow and fear that surround this event, particularly in our Western civilization. We look upon death as the greatest tragedy and feel we must hang onto this *physical* existence at all costs. We even try to keep the body alive artificially when it is old and tired and longing for release. We are imbued with the belief that as long as there is "life" there is hope, so we make every effort to keep the physical body alive.

Our efforts to hold on to life are concentrated on *physical* existence, for we identify with it even though we believe ourselves to be more than this body. But life is not limited to physical existence. It seems, then, that in order to understand what death is, we must first try to understand what life really is and what it encompasses, so that we can put the event we call death in its truer perspective.

Life and Death as a Cycle

To begin doing this, let us use an analogy. Suppose a friend were to ask you to draw a line representing life. You would probably think it a fairly simple task. You might put a point on a sheet of paper and call it Birth. Then you would draw a straight line to another point and call it Death. Life would be the line between birth and death.

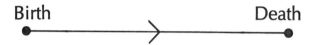

Suppose next you were asked to draw another line, this time representing a journey from New York to London. Again you would mark a point *NY* for New York and another point *L* for London, and draw a straight line joining them.

But you know quite well that the journey from New York to London is not a straight line. It is part of the circular journey you would make if you continued *around* the world and returned to your starting point.

Well, in exactly the same way, when we draw the line representing life, we should draw it as a circle— the visible, physical arc is part of an invisible, continuing circle. It could be illustrated as shown on p. 98, a small portion of a greater journey, instead of the final starting and ending of a brief trip.

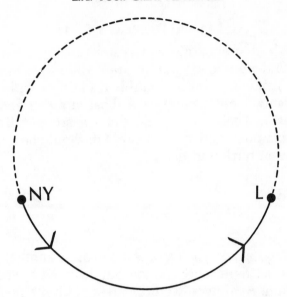

If you were stationed on an island in the mid-Atlantic and a ship appeared, you would see it first on the horizon as a tiny point, scarcely moving. As it came closer it would appear to be traveling faster and growing larger. Finally, when it came closest to your island, it would appear to be going full steam ahead. Then, after a while, it would get smaller and seem to slow up, finally to disappear on the horizon and vanish from your sight. But it would still be on its journey, although no longer visible to you.

Now, we can look at life not just as we see it between birth and death, but rather as we have looked at this journey of a ship. Very little of life appears to express itself in newborn children, but as they go through childhood into youth, there is an increasing surge of activity. They appear to be going faster, experiencing more and more of life. Finally they reach that stage of intensity where they seem to have come

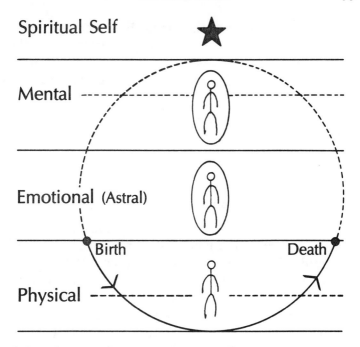

to the maximum, and life is at its fullest. We often say people are "at their prime" when this stage is reached. Then, toward old age, they slow down; they withdraw more and more from physical activity; they become more inturned and reflective. Finally they reach the point where they withdraw completely. So we can see that death is really a gradual process that begins somewhere around middle age, when we have reached our prime, the maximum of our intensity in our rushing out toward physical experience which this life is.

Death begins when we turn away from this outer activity to a more reflective experience. Death is really the gateway to a fuller, freer *life,* on an ocean that is less bounded; it is a continuation of the journey on that invisible part of the great circle. If we are dead at all, we are dead here! We are chained in the prison-house of the flesh. We are entombed (encased) in this dense physical body, the greatest limitation; and when we finally fulfill the hunger for experience at this level, we are ready and willing to be released. We are like the slave of whom Longfellow wrote:

> Death had illumined the land of sleep,
> And his lifeless body lay
> A worn-out fetter that the soul
> Had broken and thrown away.

If we have to grieve at one event and rejoice at the other, we should reverse our present practice. We should grieve when we have to come into the limitation, and rejoice when the time of freedom arrives. However, there is another aspect to be considered. For this is the part of the journey where we develop the power of *will*, which operates particularly in the physical world. Eventually, this true spiritual principle which we call *will* has to express itself perfectly in densest matter. Physical experience is a necessary part of spiritual evolution, and therefore is as important a part of the cycle as the rest of the circle in the diagram.

The Death Experience

A few words about the time of death seem necessary at this point. At the actual moment of death, the individual is seldom conscious at the physical level. The life forces withdraw from the extremities and gradually center in the heart. From there they move on to a center in the head before they withdraw completely. This moment just before consciousness withdraws completely is an extremely important one because at that time there seems to be a flash in which the whole of our physical existence passes in review before us. We see our whole lifetime in proper perspective; we see just what we have done and what we could have done better. We see the things we have accomplished before withdrawing completely and before breaking the silver cord. After that there is no further link with the physical body, and we cannot ever come back into it.

It is interesting how often we read accounts of this experience, written by people who have come close to death. People experience this flash of memory, this review of events, when near drowning. They will say something like this: "My whole life seemed to pass before my eyes in a flash, and I remembered things I had forgotten about completely."

Since death is only a withdrawal from the body, we do not go to some strange new place. There is nothing unfamiliar about our surroundings because consciousness has already focused in them every night during sleep. In fact, death and sleep have often been spoken of as twins. The only difference between the two is that we are recalled into the body from sleep, but in death the cord or magnetic link is broken completely, and return to the physical body is no longer possible. Death, like going to sleep, changes nothing about us except that we have dropped our densest vehicle. There are the same desires, the same interests, the same friends, the same activities. We are not any different when we drop our densest body, except that we are free of its limitations. We may feel and look younger and more vital than we did when limited by a body that had grown old or incapacitated through long illness.

The After-Death State

What is life like, then, at this level of being? That depends entirely on what our desires and feelings had been while we were in the physical body, because they have not changed. If our desires have all been of the lustful type requiring a physical body to satisfy them, if our philosophy has been "eat, drink, and be merry," we have a problem because, after all, we cannot eat, drink, or be very merry without a physical body. So there is sure to be a period when desires are strong but there are no means to satisfy them. This experience might be called hell. However, even individuals who experience such unsatisfiable desires make progress, because the desires wear out in time, just as they do if we control them while in the physical body. We become free of the handicap of such desires and do not carry them with us into another life.

What about people such as you and me? What would our life be like without a physical body? First, have you ever realized what a lot of time and energy are required to care for a physical body? Most of us spend about eight hours a day working to earn the money to feed, house, clothe, and provide for other needs of this physical body. We spend an hour or so transporting it to and from work. We spend two or three hours feeding it, and if we are the ones who prepare the food and clean up afterward, we use even more time. We spend an hour or so grooming and dressing the body, making it presentable. Then we have to rest the thing for about seven or eight hours of every twenty-four, so that if we can manage to find an hour or so to do the things we really want to do, the body is often too tired to do them.

Now think what life would be like without the physical body. No pain, no fatigue, complete freedom for those avocations and interests we have always wanted to pursue: to attend an opera, travel, see the beauties of nature in Australia or South America, do things for which we never had time or money. Once we are free of the physical body, we can fulfill every such desire. How, then, can we grieve for those who have reached that moment when they can move into this realm of being? I am not saying we should all go out and get rid of our physical bodies right away. They are hard to come by, hard to train, and hard to bring to the stage where they are useful servants to us. We should use them to the utmost and welcome every experience that can help us toward fulfillment, help us to give service to humanity. But when the time comes, and the saturation point is reached, we should be just as ready to be released from them.

Eventually all desires are exhausted, and we go through what might be called a "second death," in the sense that the emotional body too drops away. Then we are clothed only in mental matter, and in this finer vehicle we enter the realm of mental consciousness. This is often referred to as the "heaven world." Now, heaven is not a place, but a *state of consciousness*. It is not a dream, but a reality beyond description, since we find it difficult to think in terms of its reality. The great mystics from the beginning of time have tried to find suitable words to describe this state of bliss. They use all the superlatives, but say it is still impossible to describe such a state of consciousness. Every individual's cup is filled to overflowing. Some may bring small cups, some large, but whatever the capacities, every cup is filled because everything is there. There is only one limitation—our capacity to respond to this world. All those interests which uplift, such as the arts, the sciences, all aspirations, as it were, form windows through which we can see. Every high aspiration, every feeling of pure love is able to find expression. Truth, beauty, and happiness are there to uplift and to heal, to restore the soul and to reorient the individual after his lifetime of experience. The richness and extent of this level of being is dependent on ourselves, on what our interests are, and on what we have experienced in our lifetime.

Nothing of a gross nature, such as selfishness, greed, sorrow, is possible at this level because the rate of vibration in which these things express themselves is unable to manifest here; they are too coarse for this rare atmosphere. This is the stage at which we distill the essence of our finest life experiences and build it into the capacity for better and fuller expression in the next life. Eventually this refining process is concluded. All interests and aspirations, all pursuit of truth, and all the highest capacities generated during our physical lives have found fulfillment, and we are ready to go through a third death. We drop off our last mortal vesture, the last garment of the personality, the lower mental body, and return to our own true home with no limiting vehicles of matter.

The Return to Life

The duration of our rest depends on ourselves. Eventually a hunger for experience arouses us and we want to gather round ourselves a new set of bodies. First, we gather mental matter which will become our mental body, then emotional matter to form our emotional body, and then we are ready to receive a new physical body to pursue our new life experiences.

In the after-death period we see a true working out of the law of karma, or the law of cause and effect. There is no reward or punishment that comes from outside ourselves. We are all limited by our own interests and aspirations during earth life. What our experiences will be depends entirely upon ourselves. The whole process can be likened to eating, and this also gives us some idea of the time involved. Out of the twenty-four hours of the day, how many are spent in the actual process of eating? Two or three at the most, sometimes less in these days of hustle and bustle. These hours can be compared to that part of the cycle spent in the physical body, the actual experience of life on earth. But the time it takes to digest the food is longer, though we are usually not aware of the digestive process, unless we have overindulged. Just as unwise eating and drinking causes indigestion, there is a price to pay for unwholesome living when we enter the emotional realm after absorbing the physical experiences. There is the process of assimilation, too, and this of course is comparable to the longer period in the mental realm, where we reap the harvest of our experiences and absorb their essence.

One woman, on hearing about the process of death and rebirth, said, "I will have none of it. I will have no part of anything that tells me I have to come back. I never want to see this world again!" And, on another occasion, a man asked, "Why do we ever want to come back anyway?" Well, the analogy of eating applies to those reactions too, for think how often you have got up from a Christmas or Thanksgiving dinner and said, "I never want to see food again!" An emphatic statement—but isn't it amazing how hungry you are again by dinnertime the next day?

So we can tell the woman who never wants to come back, "There is one thing sure. No one and no thing can possibly bring you back here but yourself. You will never come back until you want to come." And we can tell the man that, as it is with returning hunger of the physical body for more food, so it is with the hunger for life. That hunger, too, will return, and we shall want to come back again and again until we have had *all* the necessary experience and have unfolded all our capacities.

Then we shall hunger no more and come back no more.

For Further Reading:

The Other Side of Death, by C. W. Leadbeater
Our Last Adventure, by E. Lester Smith
A Practical Guide to Death and Dying, by John White
The Transition Called Death, by Charles Hampton
Death, The Final Stage of Growth, by Elisabeth
　Kubler-Ross

10

The Power of Thought

The first essential in understanding something of the power of thought is to realize that it is a *force*. Because we cannot see it or hear it, we are likely to forget this fact and, consequently, think it is not important. We have grown accustomed to the idea that only what we contact with our five senses has reality. Science may have been responsible for getting the mass of humanity into this frame of mind, but science has now gone way beyond such a simple idea. Einstein said that if we are to know anything of reality "we must transcend the rabble of the senses."

Thoughts as Vibrations

Wherever you are at this moment, all kinds of waves are present of which you are completely unaware. But if there is a radio or a television set in the room, it can be adjusted so that you hear the music, the talks, the jokes, and the inevitable commercials that are in the silent waves. These waves are passing through the place you are right now, but they are not impinging on your consciousness because they are beyond the range of your senses.

Thought too is a real force, a real power, like X-ray or radio, or any other set of waves of which human beings have only recently become aware. Thought can be visualized as waves or vibrations in the stuff that makes up the mental world. The mental body, like the physical body, is subject to the force of habit. If we accustom it to vibrate in certain ways, it will have a tendency to repeat those same vibrations more frequently and more easily in the future. For example, criticizing and finding fault is such an easy habit and so common in our daily world of activity that we hardly realize how we have accustomed ourselves to it. In the Western world, too, emphasis has been placed on the critical and analytical faculties of mind, so it is easy to carry these over into our personal habits of thought. What are our general topics of conversation? We discuss what is *wrong* with politics, *wrong* with education, *wrong* with other groups, *wrong* with the weather, and so on. So it becomes easy to observe what is *wrong* with people we meet, unless we deliberately begin to cultivate a new kind of thought habit.

In the book we mentioned earlier, *At the Feet of the Master,* it is simply yet strongly stated: "In everyone and in everything there is good; in everyone and in everything there is evil. Either of these we can strengthen by thinking of it." Have you ever had the privilege of being with someone who thinks you are a wonderful individual? What does this do for you? Doesn't it make you try your utmost to be that kind of person? You see how simple it is—so simple that we pay little attention to it generally; yet if we could continually control our thinking and move it in that one constructive direction alone, we could transform ourselves and all those with whom we come in contact. If enough of us do it, we can transform the world!

Constructive Thinking

Another thing we must constantly remember is that negative, destructive thinking stimulates a response from the lower emotions. For instance, if you start thinking of an unkind thing someone has supposedly said about you, or some unkind act done to you, and then allow your mind to dwell on it, you can work yourself up into a state of real emotion. This is the way much of our group prejudice is built up. If we become critical of a certain group of individuals and then watch for anything they do that is wrong, allowing lower emotions to react to our thoughts, we soon find ourselves hating that group. Then we infect others with that hate. Thus we are helping to strengthen the forces of prejudice—religious, racial, national—which lead to war and all the other destructive and unpleasant things that we have in the world today. We could reverse the process and use this power constructively to promote peace and good will toward all mankind.

One way to use the mind constructively is to build or unfold the various virtues in our nature so that the world is a better place because we are the best we can make ourselves and therefore easier to live with. As quoted earlier, Annie Besant said: "God's thought makes Universes; your thought makes yourself; it is the one creative force by which you shape, mould, and build your character."

It is important, therefore, to look at ourselves, to see how we use or misuse thought force in our daily lives. It has been stated that we never speak, never act unless we have first thought, first made an image of what we are going to say or do. We are not usually aware of this because the thought process is so rapid.

Our consciousness is such unknown territory to most of us that we do not know what our mental processes are. But some hold that even the lifting of an arm or a finger has to be imaged in the mind before the act takes place. This is a startling idea to many people and one we should think about seriously. How often we say, "I didn't mean to do it; I just did it without thinking." Or "Now why did I say that? It just popped out of my mouth without my even thinking about it." Yet we are told this is not so.

We never speak or act unless we have first thought. The thought that precedes action does not refer to the brain processes which *can* become automatic but to the mental processes which go on in the mental vehicle. When we think, we make an image, a form, and pour into that form creative energy or force, which must result in action. Sometimes a number of repeated thoughts are necessary before the sum total of that energy is sufficient to express the action in the physical world, but thought becomes habitual, and many times in our lives we become powerless to resist the force which we ourselves have created with our uncontrolled thinking.

Most people ignore their imaginings and day-dreams, feeling these do not matter because they cannot be seen; they are not tangible. In reality they are the one and only danger, because nothing comes about in our own lives or in the world until it has first been thought. Strong desires may be felt, but it is only thought that brings about action—only when we have pictured ourselves giving way to those desires does the trouble begin.

Controlled Thinking

Let us take an example. Suppose I have become so addicted to eating candy that the habit has become a vice. I decide I am going to stop eating candy. As long as I can control this creative imagination of mine to the point of never picturing myself eating the candy, it is easy. The piece of candy, which is the object of desire, has no effect on me whatsoever. But what happens? I go down the street, perhaps walk past an attractive candy store, or a friend comes along and offers me some candy. Immediately the uncontrolled imagination gets to work. I picture myself enjoying the candy. I can practically taste it in my imagination, and I begin to think of all the good reasons why I should take it. I mustn't hurt my friend's feelings; or it's only a little piece, not many calories. Or my energy is low and everyone knows that sweet foods are quick energy builders.

We can always think of plenty of reasons once we allow the mind to begin working on it. Had I really wanted to quit eating candy, or smoking cigarettes, or drinking alcohol, or indulging in any other sensual excess, I would never have allowed a picture of such acts to enter my mind. Every time it tried to enter, I would deliberately turn to some other thought which I, the Self, had decided on beforehand.

Take another example. There is some particular thing that I have decided I should like to do. Perhaps it is spring and I have decided to get up an hour earlier and work in the garden, or perhaps study something while my mind is fresh. I set the alarm and go to bed. Now as long as I control my imagination, it is easy.

The alarm goes off and I get up and do whatever I planned. But what usually happens? The alarm goes off and the uncontrolled imagination gets to work. "It's a cold morning," or "I didn't get to sleep early, and I need sleep." If we really want to control our actions, we have to control this mind first. It is the mind that causes our troubles and makes our difficulties. The work of the will is needed to control the mind, so as not to allow unwanted thought forms to enter.

There is another factor very important as far as mind is concerned. We sometimes forget that to use any power effectively we must be able to turn it off as well as to turn it on. Thought power is like any mechanical power—like that of a car, for instance. You must be able to turn on the engine, direct the car to its destination, and then turn off the power. To let the mind go running on and on without directing it is like driving the car up to the garage door and leaving the motor running all night. The petty worries we indulge in that cause our sleeplessness at night simply mean that we do not know how to turn off the engine. If we have a problem to solve, we should concentrate all our energy and all our mental capacity on that problem. But when we have done all the thinking we can, we should be able to turn off the switch in the mind, just as we turn off the car's engine, and let the mind rest. I, the Self, must be in control in order to do this.

We can take another example of uncontrolled imagination at work. Much ill health is the result of thought used destructively rather than constructively. Doctors are alert for what they call "psychosomatic causes"—negative thought and emotion that affect our physical condition. This does not necessarily mean that all illness is caused by uncontrolled thought, although some people believe that to be so. But it is important to examine our thought patterns as they are formed in the mind.

A recent medical journal described a case of a woman who went through all the symptoms, the pain, the agony of death from cancer, yet when an autopsy was performed, she did not have one single malignant cell in her body. She created the illness and even her death by uncontrolled imagination. Many doctors would not consider that story extraordinary, but could relate other instances, less drastic but almost as unbelievable, of illnesses brought on by uncontrolled imagination.

Most of us do not go to such extremes. But the next time you experience a little scratching in your throat, or have the sniffles, see what your thinking is. Observe your thought patterns and see whether you are picturing yourself down in bed with a bad cold or whether you are able to control the creative power of thought and use it constructively to build good health.

How We Influence Others

The greatest reason for learning to control the power of thought and use it correctly is our effect on others. Most of us have learned to control ourselves to the point where we do not knock people down if they do something we do not like. Some of us even have sufficient control not to say anything unkind—at least to the face of another. But what about our thought? We must try to keep in mind that this is a real force and does a great deal more damage to the subtler vehicles than any physical blow we might deal the person.

What is our thinking when we read headlines in the paper? Perhaps it is a wonder that persons who make

mistakes or commit petty crimes that make the headlines are ever able to go straight again or do anything
right or constructive. Millions of people over the
whole nation read about their misdeeds and concentrate thought energy, and often lower emotions, on
the unfortunate individual. Let us not forget that all
of us who so use our thought are partly responsible
for the acts. Our misuse of this power of thought will
return on us like a boomerang.

The world as it is at the present time is the sum total
of the thought of all of us, and the only way we can
change it is first to change our own thinking. We
always long for some other power. We think that if
we just had a million dollars, or maybe psychic
powers, or were in some position of authority, what
wonderful good we could do for humanity. We all
have within ourselves the power to help in a much
more worthwhile way whenever we bother to use our
thought constructively; in fact we are already using
or misusing it all of the time.

In her book *Thought Power*, Annie Besant says one
of the finest things written on this subject:

> Thus we may learn to utilize these great forces that
> lie within us all, and to utilize them to the best possi-
> ble effect. As we use them they will grow until, with
> surprise and delight, we shall find how great a power
> of service we possess.... We cannot help thinking to
> some extent, however weak may be the thought-cur-
> rents we generate. We must affect those around us,
> whether we will or not; the only question we have to
> decide is whether we will do it beneficially or mis-
> chievously, feebly or strongly, driftingly or of set pur-
> pose.... Here lies our choice, a choice momentous for

ourselves and for the world: Choose well; for your choice is brief and yet endless.

For Further Reading:

Healers and the Healing Process, by George W. Meek
Imagery in Healing, by Jeanne Achterberg
Spiritual Aspects of the Healing Arts, ed. Dora Kunz
Thought Forms, by Annie Besant and C. W. Leadbeater
Thought Power, by Annie Besant

11
Meditation

Meditation is practical psychology in the real sense of that word, for psychology means the science or the study of the soul. True meditation is based on the principle that you *are* a spiritual being who *has* a body and personality through which you gather experience and through which you gradually learn to express your spiritual powers in these worlds of form. When you have learned to do this perfectly, you will have reached the end of the human pilgrimage; you will have realized the purpose of what made you human. The whole of your personality will then be in complete harmony with the "Inner Ruler Immortal, seated in the heart of all beings." Then your true self will express itself through your bodies in strength and grace (physical); affection, compassion, and devotion (emotional); and in noble thoughts and wisdom (mental).

Meditation for Character Improvement

There are many forms of meditation which will help a student to move more easily and rapidly toward this goal of true Self-expression and inner harmony. One method starts by looking at oneself objectively and trying to see the deficiencies of personality which block the spiritual Self from full expression. Perhaps one may see irritability, selfishness, sensuality, jealousy, or some other faults as obstacles. Having seen them, one must then set about weakening or removing them, and here one must avoid a common danger. Thinking about anything will strengthen it. Thinking about one's shortcomings will strengthen them. One must look therefore for the needed virtue or positive attribute and think of that. Using the creative power of imagination and thought, one can build a virtue into a living quality in which its complementary weakness will dissolve.

Many students have found the following exercise a practical way to do this. Suppose you wish to replace irritability by an inner serenity and calm, something very much needed by many in these days of rush and tensions. Set aside a few minutes each day when you can be alone and undisturbed. The early morning, after bathing, has been found a suitable time by many. Sit quietly, in a comfortable position, with the back erect and the body at ease, neither tense nor slumped. Now quietly and deliberately think of yourself and your whole personality as filled with an inner serenity which nothing can disturb. Be aware of the absolute stillness and peace which subtly interpenetrate the worlds of form and action, a stillness which is eternal and ever present, even in the most tumultuous storms of nature or of human activities. Be aware of this at the heart of your being and let its stillness permeate your whole personality. Having done this for a few moments, go about your daily work. If you repeat this exercise daily, the quality of calmness will gain life and strength and grow within you.

Suppose now, as is quite likely to happen, after a day or so you find yourself in circumstances which, in the past, have frequently upset you. What will happen? Probably just what has happened in the past—irritability will take over again. This is quite natural and should not discourage you. The habit of reacting in this way has probably been established by many such reactions repeated over a long time, and you would be a very remarkable person indeed if, by one or two moments of thought, you could overthrow a habit of perhaps many years' standing.

However, as you seek to build the quality of serenity by this method, you have two great advantages. First, you are using deliberately planned thought against a habit formed by random, haphazard responses. Second, deliberate attempts to control and use your own thought power will bring into expression the serenity of your own spiritual Self with its enormous capacity for bringing about transformation. Therefore, although on this early occasion the old habit may first break out again as irritability, you may observe a difference. It may well be that even at this early stage you will more quickly recollect yourself and find yourself saying, "I was going to remain calm and serene," and you will find that you can more readily calm yourself because of the strength you are building into your nature. If this happens you are making good progress.

Continue the practice. Every day give added strength to the image of yourself as serene and at peace. If possible keep the daily rhythm unbroken, for daily rhythmic impulses will keep the image and inner force center growing steadily, whereas omissions allow what has been built anew to decay or become overgrown, and the work must be done afresh before further progress is possible.

If you work regularly at this exercise, you will pass through several stages. After the stage described above you may find that, in the old annoying circumstances, you may give way to irritability and then suddenly recollect yourself in the middle of an outburst and find, to your pleased surprise, that you are able to control and calm yourself. Then you may reach the stage where you can recognize the rising inner tensions and control them *before* any outburst occurs. Finally, by regularly strengthening the image of yourself as radiating serenity and calm from this innermost stillness, you will reach the stage where this becomes your natural expression, and you will have built this quality into your nature. The old weakness has been crowded out and starved through lack of life-giving thought and energy.

This method can be used to replace any weakness with its opposite strength. However, many have found that thus to contact a center of inner stillness is to be aware of that which is the source of all right thought, feeling, and action. The exercise is simple yet effective. You can test it for yourself and demonstrate the power of your own creative thought and imagination.

All qualities are linked together. When one works on a quality that is weaker than the rest, it will be relatively easy to draw it up to the level of the others; their presence will help it grow. When, however, one seeks to push some quality ahead of the rest, its further development will require strengthening the others. For instance, as an inner serenity is attained, it will be more and more necessary to develop an in-

ner strength so that outer storms cannot push one off
balance. It will be essential also to achieve imperson-
ality about circumstances so that many forces which
might otherwise destroy the inner stillness will find
no reaction in the personality and so pass by harm-
lessly.

A Nature Meditation

Nature lovers have found the following meditation
helpful:

By appreciating the beauties of Nature's elements,
Earth, Water, Air, Fire and Ether, we contact the
beauties of the spiritual realms to which they correspond and which, through them, reflect their beauty
and power in the physical world.

Appreciate the beauty and power of Nature's great
element Earth. Appreciate its strength and solidity, its
definiteness of form.

Plants and trees stand securely rooted in earth. It is
the platform on which all things live. Its vast, dark domain extends far beneath us, awesome in its solid
strength.

In earth's depths, crystals, gems and jewels are
formed, sparkling droplets of earth's beauties.

Earth's mountains rise majestically and stand unchanging through sun and storm, serene, majestic,
steadfast.

Contemplate these things and offer thanks to Nature
for the beauties of her element Earth.

Appreciate Water, flowing, responding to every
change.

Think of a clear mountain lake.

Think of cooling, refreshing, rushing waters;
streams, waterfalls, gently falling rain.

Think of the green depths of the oceans, still, yet
charged with life. Here in the element Water, Nature's
first living things were born.

Offer thanks to Nature for the beautiful life-giving element Water.

Appreciate the element Fire. Nature's great destroyer and regenerator felt and seen as heat and light.

Think of earth's great fires beneath us, seen in the awesome energy of erupting volcanoes and subterranean fires.

Think of the sun, center of unimaginable fiery energy, source of all earthly fires. It steadily radiates waves of fiery energy to earth to build, to purify, and transform.

Controlled and slowed down, Nature's fires give energy and warmth to all living creatures.

Offer thanks to Nature for the transforming energy of Fire.

Appreciate Nature's element Air. It surrounds us constantly....It enfolds the whole world, gently touching every surface of land and water.

Recall air's gentle caress as cool breezes have touched us. Recall the whispering of air as it rustles the leaves, or its singing in the pines.

Consider the vast blue domain of air above, with its changing cloud-pictures and Nature's forces sweeping through its great expanses.

Offer thanks to Nature for the beauty and vitality of the Air.

Think of Ether, subtlest of Nature's elements. Unseen and unfelt, it is in all forms of earth, water, air and fire, but is unchanging.

It unifies diversities as it interpenetrates all, Nature's omnipresent, invisible element.

Offer thanks to Nature for the unfelt presence of this subtlest, all-pervading element, Ether.

Guided by Nature, the beauties and powers of the elements shine through the forms of all living things around us.

Appreciate how the artist and master craftsman, Nature, blends them in such things as:

The beauty of a rose,
The majesty of a tree,
The grace of a deer,
The flight of a seagull,
The glory of a sunset;
Beauty is upon the earth.

These powers and beauties are within our bodies and all around us.

Let us appreciate them and harmonize them, as Nature does, into beautiful expressions through our thoughts, feelings, and actions throughout each day.

Beauty is upon the earth.

Yoga of Light

Geoffrey Hodson published a wonderful meditation entitled "A Yoga of Light." It is a practical application of the understanding of nature gained from a study of Theosophy. The following extracts from his introduction set forth the principles to be remembered by one who wishes to use the exercise:

At the heart of the cosmos there is One. That One has it sanctuary and shrine in the heart of every human being. Man's first major spiritual discovery in consciousness is of this divine Presence within, "the Inner Ruler Immortal seated in the heart of all beings" (The Bhagavad Gita). Thereafter, identity with the One Alone, fully conscious absorption "like water in water, space in space, light in light" (Atma-Bodha, Shankaracharya) for evermore in the eternal, self-existent All is achieved. This is man's ultimate goal. Regular, wisely directed meditation can hasten its attainment.

The first objective in meditation is to discover one's own spiritual Selfhood as distinct from the personal vehicles, physical, emotional, and mental, and the consciousness active within them. Devotees of a certain temperament—others might not be helped by this

method—begin, therefore, with an exercise in dissociation, seeking both to realize the distinction between
the immortal Ego and its mortal, personal vehicles and
to know the spiritual Self. To know the knower may
appear impossible to the analytical mind. The seeming paradox is, however, resolved at the level of the
synthesizing and intuitive intelligence in man, the
prophetic mind, to which in meditation the center of
consciousness is deliberately raised.

The second objective is to realize that the spiritual
Self of man is forever an integral part of the spiritual
Self of the universe, the all-pervading supreme Lord,
the Solar Logos. Man is one with God and through
THAT with all that lives. Man-spirit and God-spirit are
one spirit, and to know this truth of truths transforms
life.

The meditation which follows may be used for
either personal practice or in a group. Group meditation is directed by a leader with suitable pauses.

Preparation

Body relaxed.
Emotions harmonized.
Mind alert and charged with will.
Center of awareness established in the higher Self,
the spiritual Soul, the immortal Ego.

Dissociation

Mentally affirm and realize:

I am not the physical body.
I am the spiritual Self.

I am not the emotions.
I am the spiritual Self.

I am not the mind.
I am the spiritual Self.

Meditation

> I am the divine Self. *(Think of the Monad.)*
> Immortal.
> Eternal.
> Radiant with spiritual light.
> I am that Self of light, that Self am I.
> The Self in me is one with the Self in all
> I am that Self in all; that Self am I.
> I am *THAT. THAT* am I.

Closing

> Bring the center of awareness:
> Into the formal mind, illumined and responsive
> to the intuition.
> Into the emotions, irradiated by spiritual light.
> Into the body, empowered by spiritual will, in-
> wardly vitalized, and Self-recollected through-
> out the day, remembering the divine Presence in
> the heart, the Inner Ruler Immortal, seated in the
> heart of all beings.
> Relax the mind and permit the uplifting effect of the
> meditation to extend into all the activities of the
> day.

The same procedure should be followed in private, self-directed meditation.

Any student who wishes to use this meditation regularly should read the complete introduction and commentary in Hodson's booklet.

An alternative to the exercise in dissociation is one in expansion:

Expansion

> Mentally affirm and realize:

> > I am my physical body, but I am more than it.
> > I am my spiritual Self.

I am my emotions, but I am more than they.
I am the spiritual Self.

I am my mind, but I am more than it.
I am the spiritual Self.

These two exercises in dissociation and expansion can be used alternately or in place of each other, as the meditator finds effective.

For Further Reading:

Approaches to Meditation, ed. Virginia Hanson
Concentration, by Ernest Wood
Finding the Quiet Mind, by Robert Ellwood
How to Meditate, by Lawrence LeShan
Meditation: A Practical Study, by Adelaide Gardner
A Yoga of Light, by Geoffrey Hodson

12

Brotherhood: Nature's Edict

Everything that we create in the material world, we first create in the invisible worlds of thought and feeling. This is true of such diverse creations as a giant steel bridge, a crime syndicate, a camp for underprivileged children, a dinner party, or a symphony. All these things exist in the invisible worlds of human thought before they find outer expression in material forms.

When we know that action springs from thought and see around us conditions of exploitation, suppression, cruelty, violence, and war, we recognize that these are only the outer expressions of human thoughts of selfishness, hatred, and lust. But when we look at the other side of things and observe all those creations which help humanity, such as schools, libraries, relief organizations, the United Nations, and social agencies of all kinds, we know that these are an outer expression of human thoughts of brotherhood and good will. If we know this, then we realize that all human creations are imperfect, because our thought is a more or less confused mixture of the noble and the degrading. Yet the ideal of brotherhood is not mere sentimental nonsense or impractical idealism, but is the central core around which all institutions which help humanity are built. The brotherhood ideal is the heart's blood which keeps these human creations doing their valuable work. When this spirit is withdrawn, no matter how fine the organization, it no longer performs the same function; it becomes a lifeless shell.

Separation and Unification

Many expressions of the brotherhood ideal represent the finest thinking of the world's noblest men and women. This ideal appears in the first object of the Theosophical Society, which is "To form a nucleus of the universal Brotherhood of humanity without distinction of race, creed, sex, caste, or color." Today an increasing number of people and organizations are working for the ideal of brotherhood, and it is worthwhile to try to understand it more fully so that we may work more effectively and intelligently for its expression.

One of the first discoveries we make as we seek to understand what brotherhood is will be the realization that it is only the outer expression of a deeper and more wonderful reality which is the unity of all life.

Perhaps the best way to understand this deeper unity is to consider the creation of the universe. Many thoughtful people agree that the wonder which we call the universe emerged originally from one supreme First Cause which is the source of all. Religious people might call it God, Allah, or Brahman. Great thinkers have called it the Causeless Cause or the

Rootless Root. Perhaps some scientists might call it space, for "space is the one eternal thing that we can most easily imagine immovable in its abstraction and uninfluenced by either the presence or the absence in it of an objective universe."* This common, ever-present source is the basis for the ideal of brotherhood.

From the one source, through the process of creation, emerges the amazing diversity of our universe. This separation of the one into the many is the theme of stories of creation throughout the world. We read in the literature of the various religions about the one becoming two and then three, in Trinities such as Father, Son, and Holy Ghost; Shiva, Vishnu, and Brahma; Osiris, Isis, and Horus, and many others. Then follow further divisions, into fours, sevens, twelves, and larger numbers, ever multiplying with each further dividing element, until finally we see the world in all its diversity with forms within forms within forms. One aspect of creation is evidently a process of fragmentation or separation, ever dividing, and a strengthening of each element against all others.

In the nineteenth century, Charles Darwin placed tremendous emphasis on the process of separation as the driving force of evolution, describing it as the struggle for existence and the survival of the fittest. The obvious reality of this force and its influence in the animal and plant world led some people to accept it as the basic philosophy for human society also. This led to the adoption of such approaches to living as "every man for himself and the devil take the hindmost," "dog eat dog," "splendid isolation," and other separative philosophies.

---

*Secret Doctrine Commentary on Stanza 1.

Fortunately, very soon after Darwin's theory was announced, biologist Thomas Huxley, who saw the significance and reality of the theory of evolution and of the force of separation, pointed out that there is another driving force in evolution which works in the opposite direction but is equally fundamental in the nature of things. This might be called the force of unification or of sacrifice. It has been thought that in the early stages of evolution the force of separation is dominant, while in the later stages that of unification takes control. It has been said, for instance, that the impetus for growth in primitive humanity was the survival of the fittest, while for civilized persons it is the law of sacrifice.

The story of evolution clearly shows that the force of unification is essential at every level of growth. The generally accepted theory states, for instance, that at an early stage there were no living forms larger than the microscopic, single-cell ones such as the amoeba, living in the warm seas. As vast periods of time passed, groups of a similar type came to live in colonies where each gathered its own food, protected itself, and lived independently.

As further great time intervals elapsed, specialization began to take place within the colonies. Some cells, for instance, became tougher and stuck together, thereby protecting others while sacrificing some of their ability to gather their own food. The cells they protected passed food to them, and gradually an inclusive consciousness began to control the whole colony and there appeared the first many-celled animal. Within these creatures, each cell sacrificed its independence and self-sufficiency to become a contributing part of the larger unit.

Thus, through sacrifice, emerged a new and more efficient creature of a larger and more highly developed order. As this process continued, larger and more complex forms were created, composed of greater numbers of individual cells which could not live by themselves but existed only as an integral part of a larger consciousness.

Consider such an advanced evolutionary product as a great tree. There it stands, composed of millions of cells, not one of which could live outside the united form of the tree, to which it contributes something and from which it draws its sustenance. It is a marvel of cooperative effort. Down in the roots, millions of cells draw in moisture and dissolved salts and pass them through the trunk to supply cells all over the tree. In the leaves, millions of other cells work all day absorbing the sun's energy and using it to combine water and carbon dioxide into food for other cells. Still others provide walls for the sap canals. Any botanist could list dozens of other specialized functions performed by groups of cells, each of which has sacrificed its independence to become a part of the larger unit, a glorious tree.

At a later stage in evolution, these individual miracles of cooperation begin to be willing to sacrifice themselves for other individuals, and finally for the whole of their species. We see this when a parent animal gives its life for its young, or a wolf dies trying to protect the pack. We see it in human beings when a soldier gives his life for his country, or when a social reformer suffers ostracism and persecution as she attempts to right social wrongs. We see it when a man such as Albert Schweitzer and a woman such as Mother Teresa give their lives to relieve suffering among those unable to help themselves. This force of unification is everywhere at work as one of the great forces of evolution. Some might say that the sacrifices are made unconsciously. The fact remains that they are made; the lesser is sacrificed for the greater, and because of this sacrifice evolution proceeds and enters a new dimension.

Brotherhood and Evolution

Everywhere we see these two forces at work: the force of fragmentation or separation, and the force of unification or sacrifice. They are at work in human evolution also, where apparently they fluctuate back and forth, first one and then the other being dominant. When the force of unification is stronger, human beings come together to work for a larger whole and to build family, tribal, national, racial, and even world civilizations. When the force of fragmentation becomes stronger, and people think more of themselves than of the welfare of the group, these units weaken and crumble. As the whole human life story is surveyed, civilization after civilization is seen to rise and fall in a great procession as far back as recorded history goes. And before that, the same story is told of Atlantis, Lemuria, and the great prehistoric civilizations of an almost forgotten past.

As we view the pattern of human evolution on this large scale, elements of a great plan appear. In each of the major civilizations, one aspect of human nature is specially developed, while each civilization's subunits emphasize and develop another aspect under the dominant influence of the larger unit. Thus it is said that the keynote of the ancient Lemurian culture was physical development and growth and work with physical matter and forms. In Atlantis the keynote was development of the emotional nature, and subunits of that period developed other special aspects of human nature within the dominant emotional influence.

The current major period in human evolution emphasizes the mental nature, the mind—particularly the lower, analytical, logical, separative mind with all its strengths and weaknesses. According to an esoteric tradition, the humanity of this great period first appeared in an area north of India and China near what is now the Gobi Desert, but which must then have been a fertile land. From there, successive migratory waves seem to have emerged, moving westward and founding successive civilizations. The earliest founded the civilizations of Arabia and Egypt; the next, the great civilization of Persia; then came the Celts and the ancient Greeks, predecessors of the historic Greeks who spread their culture through southern Europe. Finally came the Teutonic, including the Anglo-Saxon people. The original root stock migrated into India when climatic changes turned the Gobi area into a desert.

Each of these civilizations had as its dominant note development of the lower mind, but each had a subaspect which was also emphasized. The latest group, whose influence is now dominant in the world, undoubtedly has both a primary and a subemphasis on this one aspect of the mind. Through this mental aspect of human nature, and with the recalled experience of previous periods in the emotional and physical realms, people of this group have built the great civilization of today. And undoubtedly, through the achievements of the mind, they have brought not only themselves but all mankind to the very brink of destruction!

There are, however, great differences between the situation today and that which existed when the civilizations of Egypt, Greece, and Rome fell. In the first place, today there is no area left from which a new race could emerge to build a new civilization. Destruction, if it should come, would not be destruction of one group or nation, but world annihilation.

Faced with such a situation, nature responds, as she always has responded, by making changes or mutations in her creations so that a new species or subspecies may emerge which will be capable of surviving in modern conditions of enormously developed technology, communication, and transportation. The adaptation is not being made by creating human beings with bodies capable of withstanding atomic explosions and radiation—that is perhaps impossible. It is being made in the aspect of human personality from which the danger springs, namely the lower, separative mind.

The change which appears to have in it the seed of that which can save humanity is a transfer of emphasis from the separative to the uniting aspect of mind; from the seeing of the differences between races, religions, and communities to seeing their unities or common interests. Everywhere there are traces of movement in this direction. Of course, the process does not take place as a steady growth. Force or pressure in one direction inevitably brings reaction which may move some areas backward momentarily, as in a rapid stream eddies and whirlpools form where some of the water may momentarily be moving in the opposite direction from the main overpowering flow, which actually causes the whirlpools by its very force.

Evidence for the new attitude is appearing throughout the world. The wonders of modern technology have tied the nations together into a "global village," so that international communication is commonplace. Ecology has shown the interdependence of all the factors in the environment and the widespread effects of human intervention, and we now understand the need to cooperate globally to improve the environment. For the first time in history scriptures of the world's major religions are published in English and it is possible to study and compare them, which leads to ecumenism and cooperation among them. There is a world-wide awareness of human rights and the need for racial integration, though many violations of these principles exist around the world. It is obvious now that problems in one country's economy have world-wide repercussions, and we need to think globally in the economic realm. The European Economic Community, the World Court, the United Nations all reflect a growing trend toward international cooperation.

All manifestations of the change of emphasis from the separative aspect of the mind to the combining aspect are, of course, very far from perfect because the thoughts of which they are an expression are still far from perfect, and the brotherhood ideal which they represent is very heavily tinged with selfishness. In some cases there is only selfishness with a thin veneer of cooperation. But progress is being made, and anyone can list evidences of its presence in science, government, business, and all fields of human activity.

The New Generation

Many of today's young people show characteristics of the new brotherly attitude. They have a keen sensitivity to the sufferings of others and of animals and a strong sense of justice that bursts out in indignation over real or imagined wrongs. Paradoxically, while their outstanding characteristic may be a capacity to work in groups and cooperate willingly and enthusiastically when their interest and sympathy are aroused, they resist violently when attempts are made to rush them into a course of action without consulting them. If forced against their will, these sensitive natures may develop psychological blocks and disturbances. Youth perhaps is bearing the brunt of the strain of transition from the old to the new and is in great need of help.

When world conditions are looked at from this point of view, the ideal of brotherhood and active work for it is recognized as the greatest need of humanity today. It also represents the quality humanity will naturally unfold next in the evolutionary plan. As new races emerge, with emphasis on new refinements and new aspects of character, the process of further refinement of the older ones takes place also. Humanity's noblest and wisest souls seem to be born now in a new race and now in an older one, to unfold now one and now another aspect of character, or to help in different aspects of the great plan. Undoubtedly, also, younger souls are similarly distributed throughout the races. Any thoughtful person can observe this.

Brotherhood and the Theosophical Society

When the Theosophical Society was founded in 1875, the world—and the Western world in particu-

lar—was at the height of an era of scientific material-
ism, religious dogmatism, and rugged individualism.
Into this sea of separative thought, the Theosophical
Society introduced the ideal of creating "a nucleus
of the universal Brotherhood of Humanity without
distinction of race, creed, sex, caste, or color." However, an inquirer who investigates the Theosophical
Society and its work superficially may easily decide
that it is only an organization which works to proclaim
such ideas as reincarnation, karma, life after death,
invisible worlds of matter, and a pathway to perfection. In this book we have set forth such ideas. And
yet no member need accept any of these concepts. In-
side the front cover of the international magazine of
the Theosophical Society is published every month
a resolution of the General Council which sets forth
the complete freedom of every member to seek truth
in his or her own way and to accept nothing on out-
ward authority. Why, then, do members all over the
world proclaim ideas such as those just mentioned?
These ideas break down the barriers which prevent
us from perceiving the reality of the universal brotherhood of humanity. That is their value.

It is almost as though, at the height of the era of ma-
terialism, humanity had figuratively shut itself into
a little compartment like a telephone booth, with walls
all round and a roof on top. The walls in front and
behind may be likened to walls in time—the walls of
birth and death which hem us in. With the ideas of
reincarnation and life after death these walls are
removed and we see ourselves free in time with a vast
period behind us and a glorious, unlimited future
stretching ahead. As these ideas are grasped, great barriers to the realization of brotherhood fall. As we grasp
the idea of a great law of justice in the moral and in-

tellectual spheres—a law sometimes called *karma*—
we begin to understand that we cannot raise ourselves
by pushing others down, that only what is good for
the whole of humanity can ever be good for the individual. As we thus realize our link with every other
living thing, the walls which separate us from our
fellows crumble. Finally, as we learn of the existence
of worlds of invisible matter and of a pathway to
perfection, and realize the oneness of our spiritual Self
with the life in all things, above, below, and all
around, the roof dissolves and we see, feel, and know
the reality of the ideal of brotherhood.

The Theosophical Society has offered these ideas
to the world, not in the hope that other people will
accept them, but because for many persons they are
like windows: through them we can see, first, the
reality of the brotherhood of humanity, and then the
unity of all life. It is unfortunate that some people have
become so fascinated by the windows that they have
failed to see what they reveal. They have made dogmas
of the ideas and thus have missed the spiritual realities
beyond them. It is as though they were looking only
at the windows instead of *through* them.

Theosophical literature has many windows through
which seekers may catch a glimpse of the vista of universal brotherhood. One of these is an invocation
which, for many, has acquired almost a mantric
power. It is an attempt to sense the one living, shining, all-embracing reality behind all manifestation,
from the submicroscopic to the universal. Slightly
modified, it runs as follows:

> O Hidden Life! vibrant in every atom,
> O Hidden Light! shining in every creature,

O Hidden Love! embracing all in oneness,
May all who feel themselves as one with thee,
Know they are therefore one with every other.

For Further Reading:

The *Enlightened Society*, by John L. Hill
The *Key to Theosophy*, by H. P. Blavatsky
Life and Its Spirals, by E. W. Preston
The *Voice of the Silence*, by H. P. Blavatsky
The *Wisdom of the Vedas*, by J. C. Chatterji
One World: A Shared Destiny, The *American Theosophist*, Special Issue, Spring 1983 (available from Quest Book Shop, phone 1-800-654-9430).

13

Life: Your Great Adventure

Theosophy is not just a system to be talked about or studied. It is a way of life and can be lived by anyone with a mind to follow it. Great and profound as are the concepts, they can be applied here and now, exactly where we are, just as they have always been applied through thousands of years. Every earnest student tries to put theoretical knowledge into practice in daily life; otherwise it is just a mental concept and will never become a reality.

Here in the Western world we have come to separate the work-a-day mundane business aspect of life from the spiritual aspect, as though the two were incompatible. We have been inclined to use two sets of values, the one with high spiritual ideals for Sunday; then, on Monday morning, we go off to the business world with a wholly different set. This splitting of values is unrealistic, for actually the material world is the form, and the spirit is the life being expressed through it. Unless there is form through which life can manifest, spirit becomes disembodied; it is denied a means of expression. And if spirit ceases to manifest through a form, the form is reduced to a dead thing; it has become a corpse. From the point of view of Theosophy, the whole of the evolutionary process is that of making the world and everything in it a perfect expression of the divine life within.

Inner Attitude

Spirituality does not depend on outer circumstances or environment, nor on vocation. It is an *inner attitude*. For instance, it does not depend on the type of work we are engaged in, but on our attitude in performing that work. We get the idea that the clergy, let us say, and business people are at opposite poles as far as spirituality is concerned. Is their occupation a true criterion for judging the spiritual unfoldment of either? Let us consider business people—those who sell, for example. Many think of salespeople as being about as far removed from spirituality as anyone can be. Perhaps there are a few unscrupulous salespersons, but suppose we consider the average, not the exception. If their inner attitude is one of service to humanity, what could be more spiritual? A successful real estate saleswoman who was also a truly spiritual person, when asked to what she attributed her success, answered, "I have never sold a house in my life. People come to me in need of a home and I do my utmost to provide them with the best possible home to suit their particular needs." Isn't this a spiritual attitude of service, and is it any wonder that she has been so successful?

Now, let's consider a clergyman. If his inner attitude is one of gaining importance or authority over a large number of people, if he is more interested in the collection box, or his salary, or the checks television-viewers send, than in being of real help to his parishioners, is he a spiritual man? Unfortunately, there are such clergymen. So, you see, it is *not* the vocation; it is the inner attitude that counts.

What about the housewife? So often women say, "Oh, I'd love to lead a spiritual life, but all my time is occupied in washing dishes, preparing meals, taking care of the family, and all the endless chores." Well, if the chores are done with a grudging inner attitude, how can she lead a spiritual life? But we have all had the great happiness of going into a real home, presided over by a mother and wife who radiates happiness in loving service, and the joy of her selfless living is felt by all who come in contact with it. She is leading a spiritual life.

Spiritual Exercise

We read about spiritual things, and some of us think, "Yes, one day, when the pressures of earning a living let up, I will retire to a mountain or some secluded spot—maybe even go to India—and really lead a spiritual life." But is it really that way? Suppose, right now, you could choose the ideal circumstances that you think could provide you with the best opportunity to lead a spiritual life. What would you choose? Many of us would choose different circumstances from the ones in which we now find ourselves. Probably we should like to have plenty of money so there would be no pressure of earning a living. We should like a strong, healthy body so it would never give us any trouble. We should like to have a fine mind, so that thinking would be easy for us. We could list lots of other things. No troubles, no problems, no difficulties—that is all we ask for. Then we could *really* lead spiritual lives! Well, could we?

How can we develop patience if we are never in circumstances which create impatience? Or courage where there is absolutely nothing to fear? And, of course, anyone can love humankind by sitting on a mountain top with frail, aggravating humanity at a nice safe distance. That does not take spiritual strength. Spiritual love for humanity is developed only when we are placed right next to the individual who rubs us the wrong way, or when we mingle with those who approach life in a way somewhat different from our own.

We develop spiritual *muscles* in exactly the same way that we develop physical muscles—by giving them some resistive force to work against. Suppose I want to develop my biceps. There is only one possible way to do it, and that is to work it against resistance in the form of either gravity or weight, or by applying an artificial resistive force. Now I feel sure that, were it possible to focus our consciousness in that biceps, we should look on all that effort as evil, something to be avoided at all costs. From that point of view, we should choose to lounge, to be fed and pampered, to have a life of complete ease. But from the higher and more total view of our entire personality, we know what would happen to that muscle. It would deteriorate and lose its capacity to function and serve us.

In the same way, from the point of view of the personality, we would choose a life with no problems, no difficulties, but a life of ease, so we could sit back and coast along. From the higher point of view of the real Self, we know this is no good. How could we develop our spiritual strength in such a life? It would be as impossible as would the development of our physical strength if we let our muscles atrophy for want of use.

All we need to do to realize our need for spiritual exercise is to look back on our own lives, and see which were our times of greatest unfolding and deepest understanding, our times of reaching inner depths of capacity and strength. We find they were always those times when we were faced with problems and difficulties that forced us deep within ourselves. Look around you at those individuals who seem to be most evolved, the fine and wonderful people, and you will discover that they were the ones who had plenty of resistive force against which to work their spiritual muscles. Annie Besant once said that she could have lived without her pleasures, but never without her sorrows: the tragedies, the difficulties, and the catastrophes that she had to undergo drew forth the tremendous capacities which she developed, enabling her to do the great things she did in her lifetime. It is not by chance that we use the analogy of the steel tempered in the furnace when we want to describe the noble virtues acquired through times of testing.

Look at your own circumstances and see what life is trying to teach you. What are the conditions that keep coming to you over and over again, that you would prefer to run away from? Look at your life and see whether you can get this perspective on it. Then you will see what it is that you are being challenged to change or overcome. Are you continually being stripped of your possessions, or being taken advantage of? Are you being made to stand alone, or frustrated in what you most want to achieve? We always think that if only the circumstances could be changed, everything would be better. We never think of changing ourselves.

Taking the Initiative

The way we cope with problems is illustrated by the story of how people first invented shoes. Two travelers were wandering through a rocky countryside, their bare feet very sore and tired. Finally their journey took them across the skin of a dead animal. It was such a relief to their tired and aching feet that one turned to the other and said, "I have a great idea. All we have to do is to cover the whole countryside with the skins of dead animals. Then no matter where we walk we will travel in comfort." The other and wiser one said, "I have another idea. Why don't we take a little piece of this skin and tie it to our own feet and then no matter where we walk we shall travel in comfort." Well, isn't it a fact that many of us are like the first person in the story? We dream of a great Utopia—we would change the whole world—everyone, and everything but ourselves.

One philosopher said we are trying to make a world so perfect that we won't even have to be good. We never reach this stage, of course, and for an important reason. There are great principles involved, and we must discover them and learn to work with them and live by them. Just as each of us must walk in our own shoes, so we each must create changes in our own nature.

Who are the people you live with? What is your relationship to them in the home? In business? In the neighborhood? Do they seem to stand in your way? Cause you lots of trouble? Make your life so unhappy that you wish yourself rid of them? Instead of think-ing, "What is wrong with them?" why not start ask-ing "What is wrong with me that I cannot get along with them and respond as I should?"

We are like a radio. As you turn the dial, you find here a station that you can tune into, there another station you can reach, but in between a lot of static. Before we can reach perfection, there must be no static on our radio band. Every individual we meet is like a station to which we can tune in. We must be able to respond to every individual and remember that life at this moment is providing us with the opportunity to unfold a new capacity, to respond to a new person.

Annie Besant has stated the attitude of the individ-ual who has understood something of the true spiritual approach to life:

> The aspirant should welcome everything in his daily life that chips a bit off the personality, and should be grateful to all "the unpleasant persons" who tread on his toes and jar his sensibilities and ruffle his self-love. They are his best friends, his most useful helpers, and should never be regarded with anything but gratitude for the services they render in bruising our most dan-gerous enemy, the personal self.

Or, as stated in Mabel Collins' guidebook to the spir-itual life, *Light on the Path*, "No man is your enemy; no man is your friend. All alike are your teachers." This describes a somewhat different attitude from that which usually characterizes our relationships, does it not? But if you think about it awhile, you will see that it is true. It has been stated also that those who will follow, Nature leads gently by the hand. Those who will not, she drives relentlessly. New lessons have to be learned, new capacities unfolded; the circumstances are there to teach us. If we do not learn with the first little circumstance that comes to offer us the opportunity, if we run away from it, then it comes again a little harder, and a little harder each time, until we finally get hit over the head. But we learn.

Trusting Ourselves to Life

As long as we can be hurt, we will be hurt. Why are we hurt? If we really think it through, we will realize we can be hurt only when we are thinking about ourselves. We spend so much time and energy and effort every day building up this little personal self that we call Eunice Layton or Mary Jones or Paul Smith, seeing that it gets proper respect paid to it, that people do not neglect or criticize it, that it gets credit for all the wonderful things it does, and so on. These are the things that cause our hurts, and we continue to be hurt until this little self is refined in the fire and becomes the pure gold of the spiritual Self, the divine reality within.

No one and no thing but ourselves can stand in our way, much as we would like to blame everyone and everything else. No one and no thing but ourselves can change us, any more than someone else can build our physical muscles for us. It is only by our own effort that we can refine the little self, and life is providing the opportunities for that effort right now. When we stop manipulating life and let life mold us, then we begin to see that it all has purpose. We do not need to seek our destiny; our destiny is seeking us. "What is for thee will come to thee."

Does this mean we should sit back and wait for it to come—do nothing? Here again, life is trying to teach us. It is trying to teach us in the words of the Serenity Prayer, to have the serenity to accept the things we cannot change, the courage to change the things we can, and the wisdom to know the difference. Although it is difficult to know when to exert pressure to bring about change, and when to sit back with patience and endure, if we watch and observe the little things of daily life, they will give us the key.

Every contact we make, every circumstance through which we pass, is providing us with an opportunity, the best possible opportunity for us at that moment of time. When we understand this, we begin to experience real happiness. We begin to discover something of the purpose of life, its great laws, and to know that they are beneficent at every moment of time. We learn to "trust ourselves to life as the bird trusts its wings to the air, undoubtingly," knowing that whatever comes to us is best for us. The place to begin is not in that far-off Utopia that we dream up; it is exactly where we find ourselves at this moment.

For Further Reading:

Mastering the Problems of Living, by Haridas Chaudhuri
A Spiritual Approach to Male/Female Relations, ed. Scott Miners
Technique of the Spiritual Life, by Clara Codd
The Theosophic Life, by Annie Besant
The Way Beyond, by William L. Mikulas
You, by George Arundale

14

The Path of Unfoldment

Let us review briefly: Each of us is a spiritual being. As that spiritual being descends into life, or incarnation on earth, it veils itself, or submits itself to the limitations of successively denser layers of matter. First it enters the world of "mindstuff" and assumes the limitations of a mental body. Descending still further, it contacts the world of emotional or astral matter and surrounds itself with an emotional body of a still denser and more limiting nature. Finally, it reaches the physical plane where it is most restricted and limited in a physical body. Although all of these instruments limit the free life of the real self within, it assumes these limitations not only of its own free will but because it hungers for the experiences which can only be gained through them, and because it wishes, through them, to manifest its divine powers in these lower realms.

These veils over consciousness, which have been variously called bodies, instruments, or fields of force, are not the lifeless forms they have sometimes been thought to be; they are filled with the life and energy

148

of their own worlds. In the early stages of the soul's great pilgrimage through successive incarnations, these instruments, with their own life forces, largely dominate and control the Self's activities in these lower worlds. Later, however, when these vehicles which collectively make up the personality have felt the suffering and the frustration which their unwise, impulsive, or self-centered actions have brought upon them and have realized that they cannot weather the storms of life alone, the time comes when they call for help and are ready and willing to take it.

This is the time when the real Self, the "Inner Ruler Immortal," begins to come into its own, to take control of its instruments and a new life begins.

The story in the New Testament in which the disciples are sailing a boat in which the Christ is sleeping illustrates this critical point in every human journey. The disciples may correspond to a person's qualities and capacities or bodies, which sail the boat of personality confidently until a storm arises. They find themselves unable to deal with the turmoil, the wind and the waves which threaten to sink them, and they call on the greater power, sleeping in their midst, the Christ consciousness. When thus called, that consciousness awakens in the heart and, with the words "Peace, be still," quiets the tempest and assumes command.

The story of the Prodigal Son also illustrates the whole human pilgrimage. In the early stages the son takes his inheritance and "wastes his substance with riotous living," following the dictates of his lower nature. This leads him inevitably into suffering and want. Having tasted the bitter fruits of his actions, he makes the decision to return to his father and to serve him. Each of us is a prodigal son. The paths of forthgoing and return in this parable correspond to the two great phases of the soul's journey: the paths of separation and of unification.

Perfected Humanity

As we look at humanity we see individuals at all stages of the path of forthgoing and the path of return. We see young souls who are still learning the elementary lessons of life, others who are more advanced; and, occasionally, we meet those who are far on the path of return—earth's geniuses, her heroes and her saints. And as we look at this vast human procession stretching far behind and far ahead of us, it is only natural to ask: "And are there any who have completed the human pilgrimage, who have unfolded to perfection all those qualities which can be unfolded in human life? Are there perfect human beings?" The answer around the world seems to be "Yes."

In India the Hindus speak of them as the Rishis. The Buddhists have their Arhats, those who have reached the stage where they do not need to incarnate again in human form unless they wish. The Christians speak of the glorious company of the saints, who have been "made perfect," and others refer to them by different names. In Theosophy these great ones are called *Adepts*—beings who have learned all that can be learned in physical, human existence. So far as human evolution is concerned they are perfect, although everywhere growth, unfoldment, and evolution seem to be the rule. It is said that at this lofty level, where adepts have harmonized their whole nature with the One Will, seven paths of future service and growth beyond the human open before them, one of which they will choose.

While we are still human it is impossible for us really to understand the nature of these seven paths, although they are quite fully described in a book by C. W. Leadbeater, *The Masters and the Path*. One, however, is of particular interest to us. It is the path chosen by those who, having reached the stage where they have completed earth life, nevertheless choose to remain linked to humanity to help it, as well as lower forms of evolution, to reach that lofty stage which they have reached. Theosophical literature refers to those great ones as *Masters*, sometimes as *Masters of the Wisdom*, although the terms *Masters of Compassion* or *Masters of Strength* would be equally accurate, for they have unfolded all these qualities to the limit of human development. These are the great ones who, while living almost unrecognized by other humans and generally secluded from the world's turmoil, nevertheless guard, guide, and protect, helping others to reach that lofty stage which they have attained. It is frequently through contact with some lofty thought of theirs that the artist, poet, musician, or social reformer receives inspiration, or that movements which shape the destinies of peoples and nations have their origin.

From this great galaxy of perfected human beings, sometimes called the Inner Government of the World, great teachers are sent from time to time to different races and civilizations so that, to every nation and to every people, the teachings of the Ancient Wisdom are presented and are available. People may corrupt and degrade the beauty of these teachings and bury them in dogma and orthodoxy, but at the heart of every religion these treasures can be found. One religion may emphasize one aspect of the eternal truths and another a different one, but the spiritual essence of them is the same. Sri Krishna, Mohammed, Hiawatha, Zoroaster, the Buddha must surely have been such great emissaries from the Inner Government.

Undoubtedly Jesus was such an emissary. According to the esoteric tradition, he was overshadowed by a Master of Masters who, through him some 2,000 years ago, gave that message and inspiration which founded the Christian faith.

Anyone who has worked in that religion knows that the Christ consciousness is a living force today which can be contacted and which strengthens every spiritual thought or action. The followers of other great teachers similarly approach the wonderful consciousness of the Inner Government of the World through the teacher they follow. Anyone who understands anything of the universality of the compassion, the wisdom, and the strength of such an all-embracing consciousness must realize that it is completely above all human differences of dogma and form. It cannot be limited to Christianity or to any other religion alone.

Wherever earnest souls turn to a great teacher with open heart and selfless motive, it will not matter on what name they call. It will make no difference whether the caller be man, woman, or child; saint or sinner; church-goer, atheist, or Theosophist; Christian, Moslem, Buddhist, or Jew; American, Chinese, Russian, or Zulu—the love, wisdom, and strength of the great teachers and that of their ministers will be freely poured to whatever extent the law of karma allows and the individual is able to receive. The *Bhagavad Gita*, describing this attitude, puts these words into the mouth of such a Lord of Light: "However you approach Me, even so do I welcome you; for the paths you take from every side are Mine."

Guidance and Self-Reliance

This is one of Theosophy's greatest and most inspiring teachings—that these great spiritual beings exist; that they constantly inspire, protect, and enfold humanity and do all that is possible to help us. But although the concept is wonderful and inspiring, it is frequently misunderstood and sometimes leads the foolish to acts of still greater foolishness. People sometimes think: "If such beings exist, why do they not tell me the answers to my difficulties and problems, or tell me what course of action to follow?" Or, "Why do they not tell the world how to solve its problems?" Everything possible is being done along these lines, but to see why the help is not apparent, let us look at the way a wise teacher works in an ordinary classroom situation.

If a teacher is inexperienced and unwise, when a child asks for help with a problem in arithmetic, the teacher may look at the problem and say, "That is easy. Put down this number, add on that, multiply by so and so, and the answer will be 573." The teacher has solved the child's immediate problem, but has the child been helped? When next facing a similar problem, will the child be able to solve it? The wise teacher, on the other hand, will encourage the child to try in all possible ways to find a solution independently. The teacher will see that all needed materials are available to the child, but will keep in the background, encouraging lines of thought and action which may be fruitful. When children thus helped find how to solve a problem, the knowledge is their own. They will understand what they have done and be able to apply the understanding to further problems. They may think they solved it easily, without the teacher's help.

It is precisely because the great ones know that humanity is developing the capacity to solve its own problems that they do not tell us the way out. But their help and guidance is ever present. They do see that the needed materials are available to every aspirant and constantly help us in ways which we, as individuals, and humanity as a whole, seldom recognize at the time. Looking backward we may sometimes see what appeared to be a completely fortuitous appearance in our lives of some event, person, or book, unrecognized as important at the time, but which turned out to be the thing which helped us at a critical period, or rather which enabled us to help ourselves through a critical period. The same is true of the whole human race. N. Sri Ram, a past president of the Theosophical Society, has said that the true Master is one who helps you find yourself. Lesser teachers set themselves up as authorities and tell their devotees what to do.

The path of unfoldment is full of paradoxes which the seeker must learn to resolve or to see through so as to recognize the greater wisdom which lies behind. One such truth that every earnest seeker will recognize is that no one can take a single step along the path for anyone else. Each must take every step by self-effort. Contrasting with this is the paradoxical truth that help is always at hand, that probably in our moments of greatest turmoil and struggle, when we are

apparently left unaided, we are enfolded more closely in the tenderest compassion, and underneath us are
the everlasting arms.

Perhaps a comparison of the aspirant to the seed and
the Master to the gardener is helpful. The seed must
produce its flower and fruit from within. No outside
factor can do anything unless the life force within the
seed, urging it to express itself, takes hold and drives
it to its full self-expression. On the other hand, the
seed may lie apparently lifeless on a shelf for years
until a gardener puts it in an environment where materials such as soil, moisture, and sunlight are available to enable it to express its hidden potential.

It is not reasonable to look for the Masters to appear and tell us what to do. Unfortunately there are
many charlatans and persons who delight in control-
ling the lives of others, who style themselves "Masters" or claim to be the mouthpiece of the Masters and
to speak with their authority. Yet there is one unfail-
ing method by which any one of us may draw the Masters' influence into our lives.

These great ones exist to serve and to help and encourage humanity to help itself. Whenever we seek
to serve our fellows, doing the work we feel to be the
most needed in that service, entirely forgetting ourselves in dedication, we may be sure that we will be
used, that some of the Masters' strength will be added
to that work, and that through us something of their
influence will radiate. The more we forget ourselves
and throw ourselves into such work, the more this will
be true. If we show that we are steadfast, realize our
inadequacies and are willing to learn, then we may
find little incidents occurring, or ideas being sug-

gested to us, often from the most unlikely sources, that will show us how to serve more wisely. If we use such opportunities, their influence will flow through us ever more strongly, and under this influence we will approach the final steps of the path of human unfoldment.

The Gospel as an Allegory of the Path

The five great steps of this final pathway are described in various ways in different religions and countries, although the essence of the descriptions remains always the same. Let us consider one of the Christian descriptions from the Bible. One of the marks of an inspired scripture is that it has an obvious, simple, and immediate interpretation which will be helpful to any reader, but that, within the outer story, there are ever greater depths of meaning and inspiration which help and challenge the minds and hearts of those who constantly find in them new stimulation and understanding. Certain keys will be helpful for these deeper meanings.

One such key shows that the story of the birth, life and death of the great central figure of the Christian scripture has an added mystical meaning when the story and all its events are thought of as symbolical representations of inner experiences within the heart of each of us as we tread the evolutionary path. Such a consideration of the Gospel account does not at all detract from the beauty of the outer story, but it is an approach which has given inspiration to many who are seeking added depths of meaning in the Christian Bible. When we use this interpretation, the first five great steps on the path of unfoldment are clearly apparent in the story of the life of Christ.

The story begins with the birth of the Christ as a little child who is to become the spiritual king. This event represents the first great step when the divine spiritual consciousness is born within the heart of the aspirant who seeks the truth and wishes to serve humanity. The king is born as a little child, with all his spiritual powers latent but ready to unfold, to guide, to bless, and to inspire the heart and the whole nature of whoever will serve him. This birth corresponds to a great spiritual expansion of consciousness for the aspirant in whose heart the wondrous event occurs.

The humble shepherds, corresponding to the three aspects of the personality—the physical, the emotional, and the mental bodies—all kneel in adoration before the newborn spiritual king. Three of earth's kings, or wise ones, kneel and offer their gifts. These reflect the immortal principles of will, wisdom, and love. All around the angels sing, while above shines the five-pointed star, the symbol of the blessing of earth's divine Ruler. But whenever a great spiritual expansion of consciousness takes place, it is always followed by a reaction, as the deadening forces of the lower worlds seek to bury and destroy the divine. This is symbolized by the violent attack as the soldiers of King Herod seek to kill the child. But the spiritual nature can never be killed by physical violence, although it can be temporarily buried and forgotten. In the story, the child is removed from danger and steadily grows and becomes strong. Eventually, the aspirant reaches that stage of the path where the next great step forward is taken.

The baptism of Jesus by John, when the Holy Ghost descends and gives him power and wisdom to begin his mission, symbolizes the second great step. The divine spirit, at first appearing as a weak and helpless little child, is now maturing and expressing its powers through the personality. At this stage, these are especially the powers of the mind which enable Jesus to teach, to heal, and to set about his work in earnest. After this second expansion of consciousness, there again comes a reaction. But this time it is more subtle than the brutal attack of the soldiers, and it is directed against that aspect of the lower nature which is under the greatest strain—the mind. The weaknesses of the mind are pride, self-centeredness, and separation; and the attack against it is symbolized by the temptation in the wilderness, when Jesus is urged to turn the wonderful powers which he has gained to his own personal comfort and glorification—a course of action which would throw an aspirant off the path. Having refused to yield to this temptation, Jesus returns to his work; and we find that he who would not turn one stone to bread to meet his own needs, now uses precisely these powers in the service of his fellows as he performs the miracle of feeding five thousand with five loaves and two fishes.

As earnest aspirants grow and express these powers, they pass through the third step, symbolized by the Transfiguration. This step involves contact with consciousness of a spiritual nature far beyond the mind—a contact often represented by an ascent of a mountain. Here the personality, represented by the disciples, sees the true spiritual greatness of the God within, although they cannot maintain that level of consciousness and are overcome by sleep. At that level, which is beyond the limitations of time and space, the divine Self is seen in its true glory and in the company of those who have trodden the path before. As the Self returns, the reaction comes; the shadow of the Cross falls on the path, and the Self sees clearly the ordeal of the next great step which lies ahead.

The fourth step includes at once the greatest suffering and the greatest triumph. It is the stage at which the lower personal nature must be sacrificed absolutely and utterly to the higher. Seen from the personality level, it is therefore one of intense suffering. Seen from spiritual levels, it marks the final and complete triumph of the God within as every last vestige of resistance or holding back is burned out of the personality, which now becomes the perfect instrument for the expression of the divine. This is the stage where aspirants must prove that they can rely entirely on the divine spirit within their own hearts without any help, either from the world around them or from outside spiritual forces.

From the viewpoint of the world, this isolation is hell. All this is outwardly represented to us as Jesus is forsaken and betrayed by those closest to him, tried and condemned, mocked and insulted and forced to carry his cross to Calvary. Outwardly, everything is lost. The most terrible ordeal of all, however, is in going through all this agony with no spiritual help other than that within his own heart, and it is this ordeal which wrings from him the cry, "My God! My God! Why hast Thou forsaken me?" At the same time, it draws the divine Self within into complete manifestation in the personality. Some students claim that the words spoken on the cross should be translated, "My God! My God! How Thou dost glorify me!"

After the tremendous achievements of the fourth step, the aspirant, now approaching the threshold of adeptship, moves among people with the power to teach, to heal, and to bless as never before. Finally comes the fifth step, the Ascension: the aspirant is taken up to heaven and becomes one with the Father.

The events of the Gospel story so considered have this added mystical meaning. It is true that for us ordinary human beings, these five great final steps on the path still lie far ahead, but even at our present level we go through rehearsals in miniature for the great event. We have our expansions of consciousness and the outer reaction where the forces around us seek to bury or kill what we have gained. We have our intellectual expansions and our temptations to use our knowledge selfishly or for personal gain. We have our small transfigurations and our forebodings and, as our capacities permit, we have our miniature crucifixions and resurrections when we are betrayed by those in whom we placed our trust and are thereby forced to find a deeper center of consciousness within. So we approach and prepare ourselves for the path which every one of us will one day tread to the glory of God and for the service of humanity.

This mystical interpretation of the Gospel story is poetically stated by the medieval writer Angelus Silesius:

Though Christ a thousand times in Bethlehem be born,
And not within thyself, thy soul will be forlorn.
The cross of Golgotha thou lookest to in vain,
Unless within thyself it be set up again.

For Further Reading

The Christ Life from Nativity to Ascension, by Geoffrey Hodson

Esoteric Christianity, by Annie Besant
Initiation, by Annie Besant
The Masters and the Path, by C. W. Leadbeater
Practical Mysticism, by Evelyn Underhill
The Way of the Disciple, by Clara Codd

15

Release Your Imprisoned Splendor

Throughout this book we have been presenting ideas on human nature and the purpose of life. We have taken the age-old concept of the human being as a divine seed, a spark from the divine flame, a fragment of its splendor that gets involved in matter. So imprisoned has it become that it first identifies itself with this matter, and thinks of it as the I, the self.

Eventually, through long periods of evolution, the divine spark that is imprisoned begins to respond, to awaken, to unfold like every other seed. In our unfoldment, we reach the stage where we can begin to take our vehicles in hand and train them so that they become a true expression for the release of the imprisoned splendor that has been too long engrossed in the prison-house of the flesh. Once we reach this stage of remembrance or awareness of our hidden splendor, we become anxious to develop the qualifications which lead to its ultimate release and to our own ultimate perfection as its expression.

The qualifications have been the same from the beginning of time and have been expressed in many ways, in many languages. They have been presented in some very complicated ways, but also quite simply. However offered, they remain basically the same. A simple modern presentation of these qualifications is found in *At the Feet of the Master,* a book we have already quoted.

So simply and so directly are the qualifications given in that book that we conclude this survey of Theosophy with them. A thirteen-year-old child can read the book in an hour. But reading it and *living* it are two vastly different matters. Many a well-thumbed copy is reluctantly discarded for a new one, and some of us freely admit to wearing out several copies without ever feeling we have yet approached the goal of perfection which it can illuminate for us.

Discrimination

According to this book, "The first of these Qualifications is discrimination; and this is usually taken as the discrimination between the real and the unreal which leads men to enter the Path. It is this, but it is also much more. . . . Men who do not know, work to gain wealth and power, but these are at most for one life only, and therefore unreal. There are greater things than these—things which are real and lasting; when you have once seen these, you desire those others no more."

Next time you have the opportunity, stand on a busy street corner and watch the people go by. Look into their faces and see how filled they are with tension, with anxiety, with grasping after something, with *wanting* something. Probably the most basic human desire is for security, permanence, peace, something to hold on to. But the trouble is that we look for that permanence and security in temporary, material things, and are therefore inevitably doomed to disappointment.

Suppose you were to ask the average young couple just graduating from a university, "What do you want from life?" The answer would probably be pretty much the same all over the world. They would most likely begin by saying, "Well, of course, we would like a good marriage, maybe two or three fine children, all of us well and healthy. We'd like a nice home, all paid for, and jobs with a future. We'd like cars all paid for. We'd want *standing* in the community—maybe $100,000 in the bank." They could go on enumerating other things which seemed to them desirable. Now, suppose by some miracle you could give them all that. Would they have found their security, their peace? Or would they, whether consciously or unconsciously, realize that all this could be taken from them? Would they think, "If we can just get better positions, if we can have a bigger home, newer cars—if we can have $500,000 in the bank, then we will really feel safe." Give them all that. Give them anything, everything *outside themselves*, and it can all be taken from them. Do you see why the first qualification is discrimination between what is real and what is unreal? For once you touch the least bit of the reality behind all this, the least glimpse of the inner reality, then it no longer matters what the circumstances, you still retain the sense of inner peace, of security, because you have found something that can never be taken away from you.

Now this does not mean there is anything wrong with trying to get ahead in the world, with having a home and family and all those things. The problem comes if we feel we *have* to have them in order to experience security. We can develop some of our divine capacities in trying to accomplish these things, but we lack discrimination if we base our sense of security on acquiring temporary, material things.

At the Feet of the Master mentions other ways to discriminate—for instance, between what is true and what is false, what is useful, more useful, most useful. "You must discriminate between the important and the unimportant. Firm as a rock where right and wrong are concerned, yield always to others in things which do not matter." How little really matters! When we look back on all this 500 years from now, what is really going to matter? All the things we fuss and fight and fume about and get ourselves so upset about—how little they really matter. If we yield to others in things which do not matter, then when a time comes to take a stand on principles of right and wrong, people will usually listen to us.

Then, according to this book, "You must be true in speech too—accurate and without exaggeration." How difficult that is for us, here in the Western world, where we overwork all the superlatives. Think of the labels on the cans of olives in our grocery stores. Have you ever noticed them? The smallest canned olives are called "large." Then they go up the scale to "very large," "giant," "jumbo," "colossal," "supercolossal," and even then we have not reached the end of the superlatives.

At the Feet of the Master further instructs us: "Be true in action; never pretend to be other than you are, for all pretense is a hindrance to the pure light of truth, which should shine through you as sunlight shines through clear glass." Why do we pretend to be other than we are? The real you is so much lovelier than what you pretend to be. Isn't it true that the people of whom we are most fond are those we know most truly as they are?

"You must discriminate in yet another way. Learn to distinguish the God in everyone and everything, no matter how evil he or it may appear on the surface." This is a helpful idea because practically all of us know certain types of individuals to whom we have great difficulty in responding—the crude, unkempt individual, the mentally or physically handicapped, or the alcoholic. If we can realize that in each of these there is the same divine seed, and remember that we have difficulty in expressing that divinity even without those limitations, surely we can overcome any feeling of repulsion toward these less fortunate individuals. It is possible to change your whole inner attitude toward an individual by responding to the divine spark within rather than merely to the personality.

Desirelessness

Next we come to a second qualification—desirelessness. "When all desires for self are gone, there may still be a desire to see the result of your work. If you help anybody, you want to see how much you have helped him; perhaps even you want him to see it too, and to be grateful. But this is still desire . . . . you must do right for the sake of the right, not in the hope of reward." This is difficult indeed for us. Even when we get to the stage of thinking that we will do something anonymously to help others, we always hope someone will discover who did it and think how wonderful we are. These things can be subtle. When we think we are doing good, we sometimes find we are doing it with hidden selfish motives.

"Have no desire for psychic powers." That is wise advice for this day and age, when so many people are fascinated by psychic phenomena. By studying the universal principles of Theosophy, you may understand extrasensory perception, mysticism, and many other human potentials, but you need not desire the phenomena. You learn that whatever powers are best for you at this stage of evolution will come to you. To get caught up in the pursuit of phenomena for themselves is often a backward rather than a forward step in evolution. There is no equating spirituality with psychism. Many of the most primitive people have psychism; even some animals have it. Seeing or hearing something not perceived by others does not make one more spiritually evolved than others. This faculty *may* be spiritual, but it is not necessarily so.

Next, in *At the Feet of the Master,* comes something we all find difficult. "Never wish to shine, or to appear clever; have no desire to speak. It is well to speak little; better still to say nothing, unless you are quite sure that what you wish to say is true, kind and helpful." That just about eliminates ordinary conversation, doesn't it? We speak so many words, but much of it is idle chatter that fritters away our time and energy; or perhaps it is status-seeking, making ourselves seem important. However—even worse—too often we indulge in gossip, one of the greatest human weaknesses in our world today, and one that does much harm. If we can only remember that we have to account for every word that we utter, idle or otherwise, we can eventually learn more control and make our words constructive. Even our jesting words have a power. We have to remember constantly that every word is a force we set in motion; therefore it is imperative to learn control of our speech as well as of our actions. If we see that every word is true, kind, and helpful, we will have fewer regrets and find ourselves closer to our real divine nature.

"Another common desire which you must sternly repress is the wish to meddle in other men's business. What another man does or says or believes is no affair of yours, and you must learn to let him absolutely alone." It is so much easier to see what everyone else needs to do to lead the spiritual life, isn't it? And to point out to others how *they* must change *their* bad habits. While all the time, if we each try to change our own bad habits, we will have our hands full and have no time to tell everyone else what to do.

Good Conduct

Then we come to the third qualification, which is good conduct. This has six different aspects. We will touch on only one or two of them.

First is self-control of the mind. "It means control of temper, so that you may feel no anger or impatience; of the mind itself, so that the thought may always be calm and unruffled; and (through the mind) of the nerves, so that they may be as little irritable as possible." This is another qualification that we can really put to good use in our world of tensions and pressures. A very good time to check on our patience is about five o'clock in the afternoon, when everyone is tired and out of sorts and wanting to go home. The traffic is heavy and everyone is inclined to be on edge. Just check yourself and observe whether you are yielding to this atmosphere of irritability or whether you are learning to be serene and calm.

"Never allow yourself to feel sad or depressed. Depression is wrong, because it infects others and makes their lives harder, which you have no right to do. Therefore if ever it comes to you, throw it off at once." We have all had the experience of being around those individuals who are constantly depressed, constantly talking about all of the terrible things in life, in themselves, and in everything else. We know how hard it is to keep from responding to these heavy vibrations. On the other hand, fortunately we have had the great happiness of being around those happy, wonderful persons who manage to radiate joy. It makes you feel good to pass them and say "Good morning" because they permeate the atmosphere with their own radiant emotional vibrations. One of the most healing things you can do, if you feel depression coming on, is to forget yourself completely and go out and do something that will make someone else happier. This will change the atmosphere for you as well as for the one you try to help.

Another of the six points of good conduct is self-control in action. "Remember that, to be useful to mankind, thought must result in action. There must be no laziness, but constant activity in good work." This, of course, is good common sense. Sometimes when people take up the spiritual life, they feel that they are through with all ordinary things. They are too busy with meditation and all the inner things to be bothered—and that is the way it seems to them, *bothered*—with doing the things that come along that would help others. The spiritually evolved individual does these things better, not worse, than the average person. He does them willingly, not grudgingly. Thought must result in action, and we must dedicate ourselves to lives of *active* service.

Other points touched on in this book are tolerance, cheerfulness, one-pointedness; and finally there is this: "You must trust yourself. You say you know yourself too well? If you feel so, you do *not* know yourself; you know only the weak outer husk, which has fallen often into the mire. But you—the real you— you are a spark of God's own fire . . . there is nothing that you cannot do if you will."

Do you see how we have come round in a beautiful circle to the first qualification, the discrimination to see yourself, the real you, and to know that every divine capacity is latent within you, as within every individual? Why limit yourself to doing only those things which are easy for you, that require no effort of will on your part? These are accomplished with capacities already unfolded in you, which is why they are easy. The next time you have the opportunity to do something worthwhile that is foreign to you, some- thing that will be a real challenge and call forth your latent capacities, say to yourself, "There is nothing that I cannot do if I will."

Love

How beautifully the book ends, having gone through all these other qualifications. For it concludes with this reminder: "Of all the Qualifications, love is the most important, for if it is strong enough in a man, it forces him to acquire all the rest, and all the rest without it would never be sufficient. . . . He who is on the Path exists not for himself, but for others;

he has forgotten himself, in order that he may serve
them.''

This is the test of where every individual, including
each of us, stands in the evolutionary process. To the
degree that we forget ourselves in the service of others,
to that same degree have we begun to release this imprisoned splendor.

For Further Reading:

At the Feet of the Master, by J. Krishnamurti
From the Outer Court to the Inner Sanctum, by An-
    nie Besant
Taking Charge of Your Life, by Ernest Wood
*Talks on the Path of Occultism, Vol. 1, at the Feet of
    the Master,* by Annie Besant and C. W. Leadbeater
Walk On! by Christmas Humphreys
The Way of Self-Knowledge, by Radha Burnier

For Continued Reading
(Books with an overview of Theosophy)

The Ancient Wisdom, by Annie Besant
Ancient Wisdom—Modern Insight, by Shirley Nich-
    olson
The Basic Ideas of Occult Wisdom, by Anna Kennedy
    Winner
The Divine Plan, by Geoffrey Barborka
The Key to Theosophy, An Abridgement, by H. P.
    Blavatsky, ed. Joy Mills
A Textbook of Theosophy, by C. W. Leadbeater
Theosophy, by Robert Ellwood

Index

QUEST BOOKS
are published by
The Theosophical Society in America,
Wheaton, Illinois 60189-0270,
a branch of a world organization
dedicated to the promotion of brotherhood and
the encouragement of the study of religion,
philosophy, and science, to the end that man may
better understand himself and his place in
the universe. The Society stands for complete
freedom of individual search and belief.
In the Classics Series well-known
theosophical works are made
available in popular editions.

We publish books on:

Healing, Health and Diet ● Occultism and Mysticism ● Transpersonal Psychology Philosophy ● Religion ● Reincarnation Theosophical Philosophy ● Yoga and Meditation

Other books of possible interest include:

Being, Evolution, and Immortality by *Haridas Chaudhuri*
Eastern insight into the mystery of being and evolution.

Cayce, Karma, and Reincarnation by *I. C. Sharma*
Explores the Cayce philosophy and wisdom of India.

Culture, Crisis, and Creation by *Dane Rudhyar*
The myth of cultural omnipotence, omniscience, permanence.

An Encounter with Awareness by *Ramakrishna Puligandla*
Study of the pure consciousness of our essential being.

Evolution of Integral Consciousness by *Haridas Chaudhuri*
A study of consciousness as a holistic phenomenon.

Expansion of Awareness by *Arthur W. Osborn*
One man's search for meaning in life.

Fullness of Human Experience by *Dane Rudhyar*
How cyclic nature of creation affects our psychic evolution.

Rhythm of Wholeness by *Dane Rudhyar*
A study of continuous process of being.

The Theatre of the Mind by *Henryk Skolimowski*
The scope and importance of our evolution.

Available from:
The Theosophical Publishing House
P. O. Box 270, Wheaton, IL 60189-0270